SILVER HILLS

ISBN: 978-0-9681507-1-9

Spa Introduction: Lori Pappajohn
Recipe Editing: Cecile Gordon
Copy Editing: Monika Gordon
Photography: Michael at www.kelownaphotography.com

Staging: Interior Gift Gallery: interiorgg@shaw.ca
Printing: Wayside Printers
            1.800.663.6432

Acknowledgments

Those that have had the good fortune to spend time with us at the Silver Hills Guest House know that we have devoted people who keep the wheels in motion. Phil, our mentor, with his knowledge and passion for health and nutrition, thank you for always finding the answer to our questions. Heidi and her staff that pamper our guests with relaxing spa treatments. Thank you Rory, Steve, Evelyn, Claudette and Darrell for your dedication throughout the years. This cook book was a collaborative effort. Thanks to our new staff Kerry and Kari Straub ND for typing the first draft. Thanks go out to Julie for her hours of word processing, Lori for her consultations and Judy for reviewing the first draft. Michael, much gratitude for making our recipes look as delicious as they taste. Heidi, thank you for the hours you spent preparing for the photo shoots. Lucy, the dinnerware and props from your incredible store were very much appreciated. Thank you, Monika, for your keen eye and final adjustments to the cookbook. To the guests that have visited us throughout the years, this cookbook is dedicated to you. Your feedback, requests for recipes and cooking tips keep us motivated. It's a pleasure to create meals for such receptive and grateful people.

Enjoy,

Eileen Brewer and Cecile Gordon

How it all began
– Phil Brewer

Remember when you were a kid - walking into Grandma's house and smelling the rich aroma of hot apple pie? Remember sinking your teeth into a warm slice of freshly-baked bread? What about tasting those first, juicy strawberries of spring?

Not only is food important to us nutritionally, it is also important on an emotional level - we celebrate life with it. Holidays are marked by family feasts featuring tables laden with mouth watering food. Couples in love dine out together by candlelight. Children laugh and blow out candles on their colorful birthday cakes. Food is part of the celebrating of life and so, with that in mind, we have developed recipes worthy of celebrating.

It all started in 1984. Eileen and I lived in a small house in the woods in the interior of British Columbia. I had the opportunity to choose just about any career I wanted. Carpentry and construction were especially appealing, but something else called us.

As we went about our lives, we kept meeting people who were suffering and who were not getting the lasting relief they needed through the regular medical system. Talking to them, we realized that if they changed a few simple lifestyle habits, they could improve their health dramatically. I'm not sure when it was, but one day Eileen and I looked at each other and knew this was our calling.

We didn't have a fancy guest house. We only had our own small home. But starting small is better than not starting at all. We began with one guest - and we gave them the only room we had - our master bedroom. That was our start. Since then we have never looked back. The response to what we were doing was overwhelming and we found ourselves continually adding bedrooms and bathrooms to our house until today we have a luxurious 12-bedroom lodge, with a gym, full spa, a dining room and cozy lounge with spectacular views of the wooded valley far below.

When people come here, they come for healing. Our approach to healing is natural and nurturing. We teach people about lifestyle changes that will aid their healing process. We spoil them with decadent spa treatments such as hot stone massages, facials and mud wraps. We love to see them talking and laughing while lounging by starlight in the hot tub or when lost to sight in the mists of the steam room. And we are happiest when our guests are relaxed, rejuvenated and smiling.

Remember Grandma's apple pie? Doesn't that make you smile? We realized early on that an important part of the healing process and of living a good life is food. Yes, we need to eat food that is nutritional, but nutritional food needs to be so delicious that is makes us smile and ask for more. So gather around our Silver Hills table as we serve up what we call Spa Cuisine food to make your mouth water. Food to put a smile on your face. Food to remember.

Why we love food

Many years ago, when Eileen and I were starting out, we sampled food at other health reconditioning centres. It seemed that some places had the attitude that food had to be dull to be healthy. Biscuits were so hard they'd almost break your teeth, and food was quite plain. Some places didn't use cooking oil. Others didn't use sugar. Still others served everything raw. Face it, if a particular diet doesn't taste good, you won't stay with it. We realized that what we wanted to offer was food that was so good you would *want* to eat it, not feel you *have* to. We decided to go for balance. So we created recipes that looked and tasted delicious then we tried them on our guests — hundreds of them. And the response was always the same: "Yum!"

We also realized that people's tastes have become more sophisticated. People have travelled further abroad and have dined on a myriad of flavorful international dishes. So in this cook book you'll find a broad sampling of tasty vegetarian recipes from around the world. And here's a point we want you to remember: The cook in the house is as important as your doctor. If the cook is providing your body with the nourishment it needs, you may be spared a host of diet-related illnesses such as heart disease and diabetes. So, avoid the doctor and thank your cook for serving you healthy and delicious food.

The Art of Digestion

Ever thought of the journey your food takes? Not the journey from the fields and greenhouses to you, but from a bean or potato into the cells, organs and molecules that make up *you*. Remember you *are*, quite literally, what you eat.

The digestion journey begins with your senses — the aroma of sautéing garlic and onions makes you eager for supper. The sight of a chocolate cake smothered with fresh raspberries and coconut cream makes you ask: "Is that for me?" Just seeing the cake starts your digestive process as you begin to produce saliva in anticipation of biting into it. (Of course it's for you!)

Presentation is key — what your food looks like, the rainbow of colours on your plate, the different texture, the way the food is arranged. It's an art. And it's an art designed to alert your digestive tract that nourishment is coming its way — so all hands on deck to start digesting.

Your emotional state plays a key role in your digestion. It's hard to enjoy a delicious meal when you are anxious, troubled, angry or in a hurry. How many times have we driven with a coffee cup between our legs and fast-food fries on the seat beside us?

Food was meant to be lingered over, to be eaten with joy and thankfulness. How true are these words: " If the food eaten is not relished, the body will not be so well nourished." The challenge of the cook, then, is to deliver the entire food experience from taste and presentation to nutrition. And that's why we're sharing these recipes with you. We'd like to talk here a bit more

about digestion, and we promise to keep it simple.

When we see and smell a delicious meal before us, our saliva starts to flow. Saliva helps break down carbohydrates and starches while we chew. When we are stressed, we produce less saliva, which means the process of poor digestion has already started — in the mouth. Here's a tip: "The satisfaction of the appetite depends less on the amount of food that arrives in the stomach than on the length of time it remains in the mouth being chewed." In other words, the longer you chew, the less you are inclined to eat. (Remember *that* every time you swallow something whole as you run out the door.)

After you swallow, your food goes on an intricately-designed journey through your digestive tract — a journey that takes several hours to transform something such as a carrot to molecular fuel for your cells.

Healthy eating includes keeping regular eating times, being filled with good emotions while you eat, giving your food time to digest before your next meal, and exercising to get the nutrient rich blood from your digestive system flowing to all parts of your body.

Spas yesterday and today

If you had attended a European Spa in the 1700s, you would have been expected to bring trunk loads of your finest apparel. Every evening you would have donned your latest and most expensive fashions and promenaded through the town with great pageantry. In those days, spas were places for the rich and famous to be seen in all their glory. Spa patrons would stay a month, partake of the relaxation and also take in concerts, theatre productions, fashion shows, dances, horse racing and gambling.

Those certainly were the good old days. Spas have changed since – but their purpose has remained the same – to aid peoples health – with or without fashion promenades! For centuries people have sought cures by partaking of the waters at springs that were thought to have curative powers. The name spa comes from Spa, Belgium, a town that dates back to Roman times when public baths were housed in opulent buildings and included libraries, lecture halls, gymnasiums and formal gardens.

Changes in spas occurred in the 18th century when European physicians began promoting exercising and drinking spring water. By the 1800's, spas added strict diets and hot and cold water treatments, which brings us to the spas of today. In any busy city you'll find a plethora of spas – or at least places that call themselves spas. In reality, many of these are expanded beauty salons where you can get your nails done, have a massage or relax in a sauna. But for a *health* spa experience you need to search a little further.

A health spa is a place for rest and rejuvenation, for cleansing, strengthening and fortifying – a place where you let time work its wonders in rebuilding your health. A health spa should confront illnesses and provide tangible ways to decrease and eliminate them. Instead of leaving with a new loofah brush, new nail colour or new botanical shampoo, you should leave with new principles to operate your life. You should leave with hope. That's what you'll discover at Silver Hills, a Health Centre and Spa that focuses on the foundations of your life. The hundreds of guests who have passed through our doors have thanked us over and over. "We never knew how simple it could be to lead a healthy life," we have heard many times. "Thank you for teaching us. Thank you for giving us hope." Come with us now as we take a closer look at what Silver Hill's Health Centre and Spa is all about.

Silver Hills Spa Treatments

Is there anything better than being pampered? Is there anything better than having someone massage you from head to toe? We know all about pampering at Silver Hills. That's our job. Your job is to enjoy every single moment of it. Our spa treatments will make you feel like royalty. You'll be so relaxed, calm, happy and revitalized that you'll be sure you're in paradise. And you are. Our treatments are straight from relaxation heaven. We know this because our guests keep telling us — and thanking us with phrases such as: "Ah… I feel SO good… That was heavenly…"

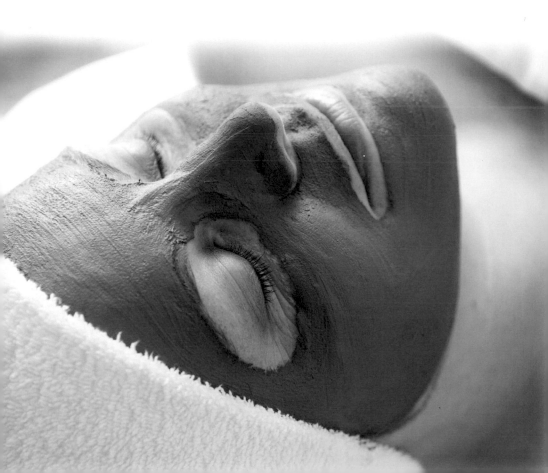

Here are some samples of treatments that await your arrival:

Our Detox Wrap is a must for those with trouble relaxing or sleeping. It calms the nerves and rids the body of toxins.

During the Hot Stone Massage you will experience the velvet texture of oiled stones as their soothing heat penetrates deeply to relieve tensions.

The Herbal Mud Wrap features a full body exfoliation to eliminate surface impurities and increase circulation. A layer of herbal mixture is then applied to the skin.

The Salt Glow uses sea salts in a full body exfoliation and includes skin conditioning oils to polish away dry dull surface cells from your body leaving your skin as soft as silk.

The foot rejuvenation is a luxurious treatment for tired and achy feet. During the massage you'll feel the cares of the world simply fall away.

So, come into our spa. Our candles are lit, gentle music is playing, the air is rich with the scents of essential oils. We just need you.

Cleansing Nature's Way

When it comes to cleansing you'll find cleansing diets, cleansing pills, cleansing formulas, cleansing drinks, cleansing-you-name-it. At Silver Hills, we prefer cleansing the natural way. This day and age, toxins seem to be everywhere — in our air, food and drinking water. It's hard to avoid them. And did you know your body creates its own toxins when overloaded with stress? Add to that the wastes your body naturally creates as part of daily metabolism, and your body has quite a job cleansing itself. No wonder there are so many cleansing fads! The body has four ways of cleansing or eliminating wastes and toxins: through the skin, lungs, kidneys and bowels. All four ways require water — six to eight glasses a day. And at Silver Hills you can enjoy deep, cold draughts of water — every drop of it is from our pure, cool mountain well. With ample water intake you are ready to sweat out toxins in our Infrared sauna, the hot tub or steam room. In addition, massage treatments bring circulation to the skin, aiding in releasing toxins. Walks in the fresh air and learning to breathe deeply help the lungs eliminate carbon dioxide more efficiently. Our plant-based diet, with ample amounts of fibre, promotes a gentle eliminatory function of the bowel. In all, you can't help but feel better once your body becomes more efficient at cleansing itself — naturally.

Take a Deep Breath

It's been said that our different emotions have different breath patterns. Anxious? You breathe quick and shallow. Relaxed? You breath deep and slow. Right now, breathe a long, deep sigh of relief. Try it several times — feel the relief and the release. If you can re-create that sigh — that breath — then you can begin to create a feeling of relief and serenity inside yourself. Try this type of deep breathing for 10 minutes a day. It's like a massage for your soul. Besides your soul, your digestion will benefit with the deep expansion and contraction of your diaphragm. And while your stress begins to recede, every cell will feel super oxygenated. Try it — starting with that deep, long sigh of relief. Ahh.....

Exercise - and your body will love you for it

We're told we should exercise. So we go to the gym to build muscles, lose weight and try make our bodies look movie-star perfect. But the main reason isn't to look good. That's a great side effect. The main reason is to get the blood circulating from one end of your body to the other. Exercise is the body's circulation pump. But, you say, our blood DOES circulate — that's the heart's task — to pump the blood around. We, and all other mammals, were meant to move our muscles and exercise as an adjunct to the heart. When you

work your muscles, they demand more blood. Blood carries oxygen and nutrients — the very foundation of what the body needs to operate. When you exercise, more oxygen and nutrients get sent around the body. Every cell of your body depends on the blood to deliver its food and oxygen. When you walk, your calf, thigh and buttock muscles act as auxiliary hearts, contracting and pumping your blood through your legs and back to your abdomen. Strengthening your leg muscles helps strengthen the heart and thus strengthens the entire circulation system. As the saying goes: "Show me a man's legs and I'll tell you the shape his heart is in." Here at Silver Hills, we enjoy taking guests for walks on nature trails that meander through meadows and woods. No need to be inside a gym on a treadmill when you can breathe fresh wilderness air, listen to bird songs, or watch a fawn frolic. You can take a break by cool waterfalls or watch the eagles soar overhead. So, let your heart and muscles pump away as you enjoy relaxing, guided walks as part of our spa program.

Silver Hills Guest House is a beautiful health retreat nestled in the foothills of the Monashee Mountains of British Columbia.

Silver Hills offers 5 and 12 day sessions as well as partial programs of one or more days.

Contact us at :

Toll Free: 1-888-547-9456

Silver Hills Guest House
29 Squaw Valley Road
Lumby, BC
V0E 2G6

Website: www.silverhills.ca

Email: phil@silverhills.ca

Table of Contents

Breakfast

Crepes

Baked Blueberry Millet

- 1 cup millet
- 3 cups water
- 1/2 tsp salt
- 2/3 cup raw cashews
- 1 cup water
- 3 Tbsp maple syrup

The night before: Bring millet, water and salt to a boil in a medium sized saucepan. Reduce heat and simmer for 1 hour or until millet is cooked. Remove from heat. Blend cashews, water and maple syrup until creamy and smooth.

Stir cashew mixture into cooked millet and refrigerate. Make the Crisp Topping and assemble in the morning.

Crisp Topping for Baked Blueberry Millet

- 3 cups oats
- 2/3 cup flaked almonds
- 1/4 cup organic cane sugar
- 1 tsp cinnamon
- 3 Tbsp grape seed oil
- 2 1/2 cups frozen blueberries

Place oats, almonds, sugar, cinnamon and oil in bowl. Rub these ingredients together until crumbly.

Oil ovenproof individual serving bowls. Place 1/2 cup millet mixture in bottom of bowls. Add a layer of frozen blueberries (1/4 cup). Top with 1/3 cup of crisp topping.

Bake at 350° F for 20-25 minutes.
Top with Pear Cream (see recipe page 113)

Serves 6 - 8

Breakfast Burritos

Great for breakfast. Prepare filling the day before and assemble in the morning.

- 8-8 inch flour tortillas
- 1-454 g pkg medium tofu, rinsed and drained
- 2 tsp vegetarian chicken soup base
- 1 cup soy cream cheese
- 2 tsp dry vegetable seasoning
- 1 cup veggie sausage, thinly sliced
- 1/4 cup onion cut in half and sliced thin
- 2 cups colored pepper cut into long strips
- 3 cups fresh spinach, stems removed
- 1 cup grated soy cheddar
- 6 medium potatoes, partially cooked
- 1 tsp dry vegetable seasoning
- 2 green onions, chopped

The night before: Remove moisture from tofu by draining overnight or cut tofu block in half and drain in a colander with weight for at least 30 minutes. Heat a small amount of oil in a sauté pan. Crumble drained tofu; add vegetable chicken soup base, and 1 tsp vegetable seasoning. Fry until golden, cool. In a small bowl, mix cream cheese and 1 tsp dry vegetable seasoning. Fry chopped veggie sausage with onion. Cool. Par boil potatoes until almost cooked through, drain. Wash and prepare peppers and spinach. Cover and refrigerate all ingredients.

In the morning: Slice thinly or grate potatoes. Fry in a small amount of oil with 1 tsp of dried vegetable seasoning and green onion. Remove from pan. Stir fry julienned peppers until they turn bright (about 1 minute).

Tear off 8 pieces of 9 x 12 inch wide tin foil and spray each sheet with oil. Place a tortilla shell on each piece and spread with cream cheese. In the center, spoon tofu, potato, peppers, sausage, spinach and cheddar cheese. Roll tortilla tightly. Wrap with tin foil and twist each end. Place on a baking tray in 350° F oven for 30 minutes.

Serves 8

Coconut Millet with Fruit

This is good to eat at any meal. Very tasty.

- 1 cup millet
- 4 cups water
- 1-398 ml can coconut milk
- 1 tsp vanilla
- maple syrup to taste
- 1/2 cup portions of your favourite dried fruits: cranberries, raisins, dates, apricots, mangoes, papayas.
- 2-3 cups chopped fresh fruit such as pineapple, mangoes, grapes, oranges
- 1 cup favourite chopped nuts (optional)

Add millet with water in a pan, bring to a boil, turn to medium low and simmer for about 45 minutes, or until water is evaporated and grain is cooked. Transfer to a bowl.

Add coconut milk, vanilla and maple syrup. Mix in the dried fruit and nuts. Chill overnight. (This mixture should be moist. If the mixture seems dry, add some contents from another can of coconut milk.)

In the morning add the fresh fruit. Stir to combine. Serve topped with a fresh fruit garnish.

Serves 6 - 8

Crepes

Crepes don't take any more effort than conventional pancakes but they do require a delicate touch.

- 2 cups tofu milk (or milk of choice)
- 1 tsp vanilla
- 2 Tbsp non-dairy butter, melted (see Glossary)
- 2 Tbsp organic cane sugar
- 1 cup whole wheat flour
- 1/2 cup unbleached white flour
- 1/2 tsp salt
- 4 Tbsp melted non-dairy butter (optional)

Tip: Use a crepe pan or non-stick pan. Letting your batter rest overnight makes a sturdier crepe.
Your first crepe will usually stick. Don't give up!

Place all ingredients in blender. Puree until smooth. Refrigerate overnight.

Heat pan over medium heat and brush with oil. Pour 1/4 cup of batter in center of pan. Pick up the pan and rotate the batter to spread the crepe. Cook until edges turn golden and top of crepe is dry. Flip crepe and cook for a few more seconds.

Remove from pan and brush with non-dairy butter. Place stacked crepes in a covered pan in 225° F warm oven. Fill with sweet or savoury fillings and serve with favourite toppings.

To make chocolate crepes, add 1 Tbsp cocoa powder per cup of batter and blend.

Makes 12 medium-sized crepes

Crisp Topping

- 1 cup rolled oats
- 1/2 cup unbleached white flour
- 1/8 tsp salt
- 1/2 cup maple syrup or organic cane sugar
- 2-3 Tbsp grapeseed oil

In a small bowl, mix above ingredients together until crumbly.
Pour prepared Thickened Fruit into an 8 x 8 inch cake pan.
Sprinkle crumbled mixture evenly over Thickened Fruit (see recipe page 38). Bake at 350° F for 30 minutes.

Note: This is a good topping to use for apple, plum and pear crisps.

Serves 6

Coconut Muffin, Coconut Millet with Fruit

French Toast

- 1 cup medium tofu, rinsed and drained
- 1/2 cup tofu milk (or milk of choice)
- 1 Tbsp organic sugar cane
- 1 tsp vanilla or maple flavouring
- 1/4 tsp salt
- 8 slices whole wheat bread
- grapeseed oil for frying

Use day old bread for French toast, slice it to your desired thickness.

Heat pan over medium heat. Add oil to coat the bottom of pan.
Place all ingredients, except bread, in blender and blend together until very smooth. Pour mixture into a bowl large enough to dip bread slices.

Dip into the batter as many slices of bread as your frying pan surface will hold. Make sure bread slices are evenly coated on both sides. Place slices on oiled frying pan and brown on both sides. Repeat dipping and cooking until all bread slices are used.

Serve immediately, topped with your favourite fruit and syrups, Thickened Fruit or Pear Cream (see recipes pages 38 & 113).

Fruit Cobbler

- 2 cups unbleached white flour
- $1/4$ cup whole wheat flour
- 3 tsp baking powder
- $1/2$ tsp salt
- $1/3$ cup organic cane sugar
- $1/4$ cup non-dairy butter
- $1/4$ - $1/3$ cup cold tofu milk (or milk of choice)
- $1/2$ tsp vanilla

Preheat oven to 350° F
Mix dry ingredients together in small bowl.
Cut butter into dry ingredients until crumbly.
Add milk and vanilla and combine well.
Pour prepared Thickened Fruit (see recipe page 38) into an 8 x 8 inch cake pan.
Spoon cobbler mixture on top of Thickened Fruit and bake for 1 hour.
Serve hot or cold with Pear Cream or Soy Ice Cream.

Serves 6

Granola

- 8 cups rolled oats
- 1 cup unsweetened, shredded coconut
- 1 cup raw, unsalted sunflower seeds
- 1 cup raw pumpkin seeds (optional)
- 1 cup almonds
- $1/2$ cup maple syrup or organic cane sugar
- $1/4$ cup olive or grapeseed oil
- 1 tsp salt
- 2 Tbsp vanilla
- 1 Tbsp maple flavouring (optional)

Preheat oven to 250° F

Mix all dry ingredients together in a large bowl.
Combine vanilla and maple flavouring with maple syrup. Combine liquid ingredients, add to dry ingredients and mix well together.
Pour granola mixture into a deep baking pan.
Bake 1 1/2 - 2 hours, or until mixture is golden brown. Stir occasionally to keep granola from burning. Cool and store in sealed container.

Makes 12 cups

31

Marmalade

Use organic oranges and lemons for this tasty marmalade.

- 1/2 cup grated fresh orange peel
- 1 cup orange pulp (remove membrane – see Cooking Terms)
- 1/2 fresh lemon, thinly sliced with peel
- 1 1/2 cups water
- 3 cups dried pineapple pieces
- 1/2 cup water

Place orange peel, orange pulp and lemon slices in a pot with 1 1/2 cups water and simmer 5 minutes.

Cover pot and refrigerate for 12 hours to infuse the flavours and soften rind.

Return pot to medium high heat and cook mixture rapidly for about 30 minutes or until peel is tender.

Meanwhile, put dried pineapple and 1/2 cup water in a small pot. Simmer covered until fruit is soft enough to blend. Pour softened pineapple into food processor and blend until smooth.

Add blended pineapple to orange, lemon mixture and bring to a boil. Reduce heat and simmer 15 minutes.

Heat 2 cup mason jars (pints) in boiling water with their lids. Remove scalding hot jars, spoon in the hot marmalade, leaving 1/2 inch space from top of jar. Wipe off the rim of jar. Screw caps on tightly, cool and refrigerate.

Yields 4 cups

Muesli

The ratio of oats to fruits to nuts is in your hands. However, oats should be the primary ingredient.

- rolled oats (old fashioned or quick)
- dried apricots, cranberries, dates, raisins, mangoes, or any dried fruits of

Your choice:
- chopped nuts such as cashews, almonds, and pecans (Do not use walnuts or peanuts as they ruin the taste)
- shredded coconut
- flax seed (optional)
- milk of choice (tofu, soy, rice)
- maple syrup to taste

Make up a large mixture of dried ingredients according to your taste and store in an airtight container. In a glass bowl, measure out amount of dried ingredients for servings required.

Top with milk until mixture is covered. Refrigerate overnight.

Wet muesli should be thrown out after the third day.

Multi-Grain or Oat Waffles

These waffles are crisp out of the waffle iron but slowly turn soft.

- 2 cups tofu milk (or milk of choice)
- 1 1/2 cups quick oats
- 2 tsp vanilla
- 2 Tbsp melted non-dairy butter (see Glossary)
- 1 Tbsp organic cane sugar or maple syrup
- 1/2 cup cornmeal
- 1/2 cup nuts (such as blanched almonds)
- 1 tsp baking powder (add in the morning)

Pour milk in a blender and add the rest of the ingredients except for baking powder. Puree the ingredients until smooth. Refrigerate overnight. In the morning add baking powder. If too thick add a little more milk to make a batter consistency. Bake waffles according to your waffle maker.

Tip: Reheat leftover waffles in a 350° F oven on a baking sheet.

Makes 6 – 6 inch round waffles

Tofu Benedict

Plum or Apricot Bundles

- 1/2 recipe of Basic Bread Dough (see Breads) or Quick Thin Crust Pizza
- 15 fresh plums or apricots
- 3/4 cup cooked, mashed dates
- 1/4 tsp cinnamon
- 1/4 cup melted non-dairy butter
- 1 cup finely shredded coconut

Make dough recipe. When dough has finished rising, roll to 1/4 inch thick.

Cut into pieces large enough to cover the size of fruit.

To make date filling: chop dates, add with cinnamon to a small amount of water in a pot. Stir until dates rehydrate and form a smooth paste.

Cut open the plum or apricot, remove pit and stuff with a spoonful of date filling.

Place stuffed fruit on dough. Join the points of dough together and pinch to seal the bundle. Brush with melted non-dairy butter. Roll in shredded coconut.

Bake seam-side down on an oiled baking sheet at 350° F for 30-35 minutes or until golden brown.

Serve warm, drizzled with Pear Cream (see recipe page 113).

Serves 15

Raspberry Jam

This Jam is bursting with fresh berry flavour and with no added sugar.

- 1 cup fresh or frozen unsweetened raspberries (or strawberries)
- 1 cup dried pineapple pieces

Mash berries with pineapple pieces and let sit until pineapple is quite soft, about 8 hours. Scoop fruit into food processor and blend until smooth. Spoon jam into a glass jar. Jam lasts 10 days in the refrigerator.

Note: If using frozen berries, place on top of dried pineapple and leave at room temperature to thaw for 8 hours.

Yields 2 cups

Thickened Fruit

When Okanagan fruits are plentiful, freeze them for winter use.

Use frozen apricots, apples, berries, cherries, Italian plums, peaches, pears

Thaw frozen fruit, drain the juice into a small saucepan. Transfer saved fruit into a bowl.

In the saucepan add $1/3$ cup of honey for every 4 cups of fruit thawed. Bring the juice and sweetener to a slow boil. For every cup of thawed fruit use $1/4$ cup of cold water dissolved with 1 Tbsp of cornstarch. Add cornstarch mixture to heated juice, stir constantly until liquid turns clear. Remove thickened juice from the heat and pour over saved fruit.

Use as a filling for fruit cobbler, fruit crisp, or serve hot or cold over crepes, french toast, pancakes, or waffles,

Tofu Benedict

- 1-454 g package medium tofu, rinsed and drained
- 1 Tbsp garbanzo flour
- 1 Tbsp chicken soup base powder
- 1/4 cup yellow pepper
- 1/4 cup chopped red pepper
- 1/4 cup chopped green pepper
- 1/4 cup sliced black olives
- 1/4 cup green onion chopped
- 1/2 cup shredded soy cheddar cheese

Drain tofu overnight or slice tofu block in half and drain with a weight for 30 minutes.

Crumble tofu in a small bowl and add the remaining ingredients. Form into desired size of patties and fry in an oiled frying pan. Brown the bottom of patty before turning it and cooking the other side.

You can vary this recipe by adding other vegetables such as mushrooms or tomato.

Serve this omelette on toasted whole wheat English muffins with a round of tomato and a drizzle of vegan Hollandaise (see recipe page 121).

Makes 8 - 2 inch servings

Tropical Fruit Rice Pudding

- 2 cups cooked rice
- 1/4 tsp cinnamon
- 1 cup canned or fresh chopped pineapple
- 1/2 cup raw cashews
- 2/3 cup water (or enough for blending)
- 1 Tbsp honey or maple syrup
- 4 Tbsp orange or pineapple juice concentrate

Preheat oven to 350° F
Mix rice, cinnamon and pineapple in a large bowl.
Blend cashews, water, honey and orange juice concentrate until creamy.
Add blended ingredients to rice mixture and combine well.
Place in a well-oiled casserole dish and bake for 40-45 minutes. Or, you may make the pudding the night before and store in the refrigerator, then bake in the morning.

Serve warm with Thickened Fruit (see recipe page 38) or fruit salad.

Makes 6 - 1/2 cup servings

Notes:

Breads & Quick Breads

Breads & Quick Breads

Foccacia Bread

Banana Muffins

- 2 ripe bananas, mashed
- $1/2$ cup organic cane sugar
- $1/4$ cup grape seed oil
- $1/4$ cup of dessert tofu
- 1 cup tofu milk (or milk of choice)
- $1\,1/2$ cups flaked cereal (bran flakes, etc.)
- $1\,1/2$ to 2 cups unbleached flour
- 1 tsp baking soda
- $1/2$ tsp baking powder
- $1/2$ tsp salt
- $1/2$ tsp cinnamon (optional)
- $2/3$ cup chopped walnuts

Blend sugar, oil, tofu and milk in blender. Add mashed bananas and blend.
Transfer mixture to a bowl. Stir in flaked cereal and let stand 5 minutes.
Mix dry ingredients together.

With a few swift strokes, add combined dry ingredients to the wet ingredients.

Spoon into lightly oiled muffin tins.

Bake at 400° F for 15-20 minutes or until toothpick comes out clean.

Makes 12 small muffins

Bannock

Every culture has some form of quick bread. Here is an indigenous Canadian recipe with a few changes.

- 1 1/2 cups whole wheat flour
- 1 1/2 cups unbleached flour
- 1 1/2 Tbsp baking powder
- 3 Tbsp organic cane sugar
- 1/4 tsp salt
- 1 tsp dried vegetable seasoning (see Glossary)
- 1/2 cup non-dairy butter
- 1 1/4 cups tofu milk (or milk of choice)

Measure dry ingredients into a bowl.

Cut in non-dairy butter until crumbly.
Add milk until dough forms a soft ball.
Roll out dough to approximately 1/2 inch thick.
Cut into 2 1/2 inch squares.
Fry bannock in a lightly oiled frying pan on medium-low heat.
Cover the frying pan with a lid to trap in heat and moisture.
This method also activates the baking powder to help create a lighter biscuit.
Cook for about 4 minutes on each side.

You can also bake the bannock on an oiled baking sheet. Preheat oven to 400° F. Bake for 10–15 minutes.

Makes approximately 15 pieces

Basic Bread

- 4 cups warm water
- 1/4 cup organic cane sugar
- 2 cups rolled oats
- 1 1/2 tsp salt
- 2 Tbsp dry instant yeast
- 2 Tbsp gluten flour (optional)
- 2 Tbsp oil
- 3 cups flour (combination of whole wheat and unbleached white)
- 1 Tbsp fresh lemon juice
- 5 additional cups whole wheat and unbleached flour combined

Mix all of the above ingredients except the 5 cups of flour in a large mixing bowl or bread mixer. Let proof for 10 minutes.

Gradually add remaining 5 cups of flour until you have a soft, kneadable dough that no longer sticks to the sides of the bowl. Knead for 10 minutes. Place in an oiled bowl and turn dough over.
Let dough rise for 20 minutes in a warm place.

Preheat oven to 350° F. Divide and shape dough into loaves or buns. Place in oiled pans and let rise 30 minutes. Bake for 45 minutes.

Turn out of pans and allow bread to cool before serving. For variety, try adding 1 cup of raisins or nuts to the dough before you add the bulk of the flour.

Tip: You can choose how light or heavy you want your bread to be by varying the amount of whole wheat and unbleached white flour you use.
Another Tip: Make the entire Basic Bread recipe. Use half the dough to make 2 bread loaves and use the rest to make a dozen buns, a tea ring or a maple nut twist.

Makes 4 medium loaves or 3 dozen buns

Blueberry Muffins

- 3 cups flour (unbleached and whole wheat combined)
- 4 tsp baking powder
- 1/2 tsp salt
- 1/2 cup organic cane sugar
- 1/2 cup grapeseed oil
- 2 Tbsp non-dairy butter
- 1 pkg (150 g) dessert tofu
- 1 tsp vanilla
- 1 cup tofu milk (or milk of choice)
- 2 cups fresh or frozen blueberries

Preheat oven to 400° F

In a bowl, stir together flour, baking powder and salt. Make a well in dry ingredients.

In a separate bowl, cream sugar, oil, and butter substitute. Add tofu, vanilla, and tofu milk. Mix well.

Pour wet ingredients into dry ingredients and stir gently until just mixed. Fold in berries. If using frozen berries, lightly dust with flour. Spoon into oiled muffin tins. Bake 15-20 minutes or until toothpick comes out clean from center of muffin. Cool muffins for several minutes before removing from tins.

Makes 16 medium muffins

Cinnamon Buns

- 1/2 recipe Basic Bread makes two 9 x 13 inch pans (see recipe page 46)
- 2/3 cup non-dairy butter
- 1 cup organic cane sugar
- 1 cup chopped walnuts
- 4 - 6 Granny Smith apples, peeled and grated
- cinnamon to taste
- 1 cup maple syrup

Make Basic Bread recipe. After kneading let the bread dough rise about 30 minutes. Spray two 9 x 13 inch glass pans and drizzle about 1/2 cup maple syrup into oiled pans. Punch down dough, then roll with rolling pin into a rectangle about 1/4 inch thick.

Spread rectangles with soft non-dairy butter. Sprinkle with desired amount of cane sugar and cinnamon.
Sprinkle on chopped nuts and grated apple
Roll into a jelly roll, cut into 1 1/2 inch rolls and place in prepared pan.

Bake at 350° F for about 30 minutes or until golden brown.
Turn out onto parchment paper or maple syrup will harden in pan.

Makes 24 rolls

Coconut Muffins

- 1 1/2 cups flour-unbleached and whole wheat combined
- 1 cup lightly toasted coconut
- 1/2 cup organic cane sugar
- 1 1/2 tsp baking powder
- 1/2 tsp baking soda
- 1/4 tsp salt
- 3/4 cup coconut milk
- 1/2 cup dessert tofu
- 1/4 cup grapeseed oil
- 1 tsp vanilla
- zest of medium orange
- 1/2 cup chopped almonds, lightly roasted

Preheat oven to 400° F.
In a bowl, stir together flour, toasted coconut, sweetener, baking powder, baking soda and salt. Make a well in dry ingredients.

In a small bowl, mix coconut milk, tofu, oil, vanilla and orange zest. Add to dry ingredients. Stir gently until just mixed.

Spoon into oiled muffin tins. Top muffins with roasted almonds.

Bake 12-15 minutes or until toothpick comes out clean from center of muffin. Cool muffins for several minutes before removing from tins.

Makes 6 medium muffins

Corn Bread

For a zestier corn bread flavour, add $1/2$ cup shredded soy cheese or 1 tsp diced fresh jalapeno.

- 1 $1/2$ cups corn meal
- 2 $1/2$ cups tofu milk (or milk of choice)
- 2 cups unbleached white flour
- 1 tsp salt
- 2 tsp baking powder
- $1/4$ cup liquid honey
- $1/4$ cup olive oil
- $1/4$ cup ground flax seed (optional)

Preheat oven to 375° F.

Stir milk and cornmeal together in a large bowl. Let stand 5 minutes.
Stir dry ingredients together. Mix honey and olive oil until well blended.

Add dry ingredients and wet ingredients together. Mix well.
Pour mixture into an 8 x 8 inch pan that has been sprayed with oil.

Bake for 45 minutes or until inserted toothpick comes out clean.

Serves 9

Foccacia Bread

This dough is very soft when working with it and produces a lovely, light bread.

- 1 Tbsp dry instant yeast
- 1 cup warm water
- 1 cup unbleached white flour
- 1 cup whole wheat flour
- 1 tsp salt
- 1 Tbsp olive oil
- 1 tsp rosemary or oregano

Combine yeast and water and let proof for 10 minutes. Beat flour and salt with yeast mixture. Knead dough until it starts to come off the sides of bowl (about 10 minutes). Form dough into a ball and place in an oiled bowl. Turn dough over and cover with plastic wrap.

Let dough rise 1 hour in warmed oven with oven light on. Line baking sheet with parchment paper. Punch down the dough. Place dough on prepared baking sheet and form into 10 inch circular shape. Let rise for about 30 minutes in draft free area until dough doubles in size.

Preheat oven to 425° F. With fingertips, make dimples in risen dough. Drizzle with olive oil and rosemary. Place in center of oven and bake for 7 minutes. Slip parchment paper out from under the bread and bake for 10 minutes longer, or until golden brown.

Serve with balsamic vinegar and extra virgin olive oil dip.

Note: If you have a bakers' tile, use it for this recipe. Bake according to manufacturer's instructions.

Serves 6

Grandma's Bannock (Fry Bread)

Yes, this is called bannock as well, but this recipe is made with yeast.

- 5-6 cups flour (use combination of whole wheat and unbleached)
- 1 1/2 cups lukewarm water
- 1 1/2 tsp organic cane sugar
- 1 tsp instant yeast
- 1 tsp sea salt
- 1 Tbsp grapeseed oil

In a large bowl combine water, sugar and yeast, and stir. Let sit for ten minutes to proof. Add salt and oil.

Gradually add enough flour to make a soft dough. Knead about ten minutes, less if you use a bread machine. Cover and let rise for 2 hours.

Roll out dough 1/2 inch thick and cut into 2 1/2 inch squares.

Heat 2 inches of oil in frying pan on medium heat.
Do not overload pan with dough squares or oil temperature will drop.

Turn bannock over continually for the dough to cook evenly. Adjust heat to keep oil from getting too hot. Fry until golden brown. Drain fry bread on paper towel to remove any excess oil.

Makes approximately 15 pieces

Italian Bread Sticks

- 2 cups warm water
- 1/4 cup organic cane sugar
- 1 Tbsp dry instant yeast
- 2 tsp salt
- 1/4 cup extra virgin olive oil
- 2 Tbsp Italian seasoning or spaghetti seasoning (dried)
- 1/2 tsp garlic powder (optional)
- 1/2 tsp onion powder (optional)
- 1 cup whole wheat flour
- 4 cups unbleached white flour

Proof yeast in warm water with sugar for 10 minutes.

Mix all ingredients together and knead dough for 10 minutes.
Let rise 20 minutes.

Preheat oven to 350° F. Divide dough in half. Place one half on a floured counter top and roll it out to form a rectangle about 1/2 inch thick.

Place rolled out dough on an oil-sprayed baking sheet. Cut dough into thin strips about 1/2 inch apart along the width of the pan. Repeat this process with the remaining dough portion.

Bake for 30 minutes.

Tip: To make a great pizza crust, roll to fit 2 medium-sized pizza pans, or use a bakers' tile. (see pizza recipe)

Makes about 12 bread sticks

Light Rye Bread

- 2 cups boiling water
- 1/2 cup molasses
- 1 1/2 tsp salt
- 1 Tbsp fresh squeezed lemon juice
- 2 Tbsp honey
- 1 cup rye flour
- 1/4 cup caraway seeds (optional)

- 1/2 cup warm water
- 1 Tbsp dry instant yeast
- 1 1/2 tsp organic cane sugar
- 2 cups whole wheat flour
- 4 cups unbleached white flour

Mix first seven ingredients together in a large bowl and let cool until molasses mixture is just warm.

Dissolve yeast and organic cane sugar in 1/2 cup warm water. Proof for 10 minutes. Add to molasses mixture.

Stir in unbleached white flour and whole wheat flour until dough is soft enough to knead. Knead for 5-10 minutes.

Let dough rise approximately 30 minutes then form into 2 round loaves.

Place both loaves on an oiled baking sheet and let rise 20 minutes.

Bake for 45 minutes to 1 hour in a preheated oven at 375° F.

Allow bread to cool on wire racks before slicing.

Makes 2 medium-sized round loaves

Maple Nut Twist

- 1/2 recipe of Basic Bread (see recipe page 46)
- 1 1/2 cup organic cane sugar
- 1 cup finely chopped walnuts
- 1 tsp maple extract
- 1/3 to 1/2 cup softened non-dairy butter

Mix together sugar, walnuts and maple extract.

Divide the bread dough into thirds, each about the size of a tennis ball. On a floured counter top, roll out each ball to form a round, 1/4 inch thick dough circle that will fit on a 10–12 inch diameter baking or pizza pan.

Place the first dough circle on the lightly oiled baking pan. Spread evenly with non-dairy butter. Sprinkle one third of the sugar mixture over the buttered dough.

Place the second dough circle on top of the first. Butter it and sprinkle with another third of sugar mixture. Repeat this process with the last dough circle, using the last of the sugar mixture.

Place a medium-sized drinking glass or cup in the center of the dough rounds. Using a sharp knife, cut through the dough layers from the lip of the cup out to the edge of the pan. Cut 16 wedges evenly around the glass.

Twist each of the 16 dough pieces 5 times. Let dough rise 10 minutes.

Preheat oven to 350° F. Bake for about 30 minutes or until golden brown.

Makes 16 servings

Oat Cakes

- 1 cup unbleached flour
- 1 cup whole wheat flour
- 2 cups quick oats
- 3/4 cup organic cane sugar
- 1/4 tsp salt
- 1 cup non-dairy butter
- 1 cup warm water
- 1 tsp baking soda

Blend together dry ingredients and non-dairy butter until fine and crumbly. Dissolve baking soda in warm water and add to blended mixture.. Stir until mixture comes together. Refrigerate at least 30 minutes. Roll 1/2 inch thick on lightly floured board.
Cut into 21/2 inch squares, or use a round cookie cutter. Place on lightly oiled baking sheet leaving 1/4 inch between each oat cake.

Bake at 350° F 10-15 minutes or until golden brown.

Makes 24 pieces

Savoury Scones

Old Fashioned Oatmeal Bread

- 2 cups tofu milk (or milk of choice)
- 2 cups quick rolled oats, uncooked
- 2 Tbsp non-dairy butter
- 1/4 cup organic cane sugar
- 1 1/2 tsp salt
- 2 Tbsp non-dairy butter
- 1/2 cup warm water
- 1 Tbsp active dry yeast
- 5 cups sifted flour

Scald milk. Stir in rolled oats, organic cane sugar, salt and non-dairy butter. Remove from heat and cool to lukewarm.

Sprinkle yeast in warm water; stir to dissolve. Add milk mixture and 2 cups flour to yeast. Beat with electric mixer using dough hook attachment scraping bowl occasionally. Add remaining flour, a little at a time, making a soft dough that leaves the side of the bowl.

Turn dough onto floured board. Knead until smooth and elastic, 8-10 minutes. Place in an oiled bowl and turn dough over. Cover and let rise in warm place until doubled, about 30 minutes.

Shape into loaves and place in oiled loaf pan. Let dough rise until almost doubled, about 1 hour and 15 minutes.

Bake at 375° F for about 40 minutes. If bread starts to brown too quickly, cover loosely with a sheet of tin foil.

Makes 2 loaves

Pita

Cut in half and fill "pockets" with a sandwich or falafel filling

- 2 cups whole wheat flour
- 1 Tbsp active dry yeast
- 1 1/4 cups warm water
- 1/2 tsp salt
- 1 1/2 cups all-purpose flour (approximately)

Measure first 4 ingredients into large bowl and mix well.

Work in enough remaining flour until dough pulls away from sides of bowl. Turn out onto floured surface. Knead 4 to 5 minutes until smooth and elastic.

Cut and shape into 10 balls. Roll out each ball 1/4 inch thick and 5 to 6 inches in diameter on lightly floured surface. Both sides should be lightly covered with flour. Place on a non-stick baking sheet or a cornmeal dusted regular baking sheet. Cover with tea towel and let pitas rest for 30 minutes.

If you have a baking tile, preheat it according to manufacturer's instructions. Bake in 500° F oven on bottom rack for 5 minutes. Pitas bake quickly! Remove from oven before they turn too dark.

Serve warm or cool with desired filling. Keep wrapped with a clean tea towel to keep soft.

Makes 10

Savoury Scones

- 1 1/2 cups whole wheat flour
- 1 1/2 cups unbleached flour
- 4 tsp baking powder
- 1 tsp baking soda
- 1 tsp dried vegetable seasoning (see Glossary)
- 1 tsp ground oregano
- 1/2 cup non-dairy butter
- 3/4 cup non-dairy milk (or milk of choice)

Measure dry ingredients into a bowl.
Add non-dairy butter and blend with fingers until crumbly.
Make a well in the mixture and add tofu milk.
Stir to make a soft dough. Knead six times.

Pat into two rounds about 1/2 inch thick (12 mm) on an oiled baking sheet.
Spread onion and pepper topping evenly over the top and to the edges of the scone.
Bake at 400° F 25-30 minutes or until bottom is golden brown.
If top gets too dark, lay tin foil over scone to keep from burning.
Cool on wire rack. Cut into wedges.

Makes 12 - 16

Topping for Savoury Scones

- 2 Tbsp extra virgin olive oil
- 2 cups onions, diced
- 2 cups red, green, and yellow peppers, diced
- 1 tsp ground oregano
- 1 tsp dried vegetable seasoning (see Glossary)
- 1 Tbsp organic cane sugar

Heat oil in frying pan. Add onions and peppers. Sauté until soft.
Add seasonings and organic cane sugar.
Cook until sugar dissolves. Cool mixture before topping the scones.

Whole Wheat Sunflower Bread

- 2 1/2 cups warm water
- 1 tsp instant yeast
- 2 cups whole wheat flour
- 4 cups whole wheat flour
- 2 cups unbleached flour
- 1 tsp salt
- 1 cup roasted sunflower
  seeds, salted or not

Dissolve yeast in warm water. Beat in 2 cups whole wheat flour. Let this sponge rest for 30 minutes.

After 30 minutes, add remaining flour, sunflower seeds and salt. Beat to make a soft, sticky dough. The dough will be quite wet; don't be tempted to add extra flour.

Preheat oven to 400° F

continued on next page: ->

Place dough in an oiled bowl and turn dough over, so oil is on top. Cover bowl with plastic wrap or a damp dish towel. Let dough rise for 45-50 minutes, or until doubled in bulk.

Turn dough onto floured surface and knead for 10 minutes. The dough will still be quite sticky.

Form dough into an oblong shape and place on an oiled baking sheet. Sprinkle the top with sunflower seeds. Cover with an inverted stainless steel bowl. Leave to rise for 15 minutes.

If using a baking tile, follow manufacturer's instructions. Form loaf, cover with sunflower seeds and transfer to a bakers peel sprinkled with cornmeal. Cover with inverted stainless steel bowl. Let rise for 15 minutes. Slide onto heated baking stone in oven.

Bake at 400° F for about 30-35 minutes, or until loaf sounds hollow when tapped on bottom.

Notes:

Beverages

Beverages

Carrot and Apple Juice, Forest Fruit Slush, Watermelon Cooler

Juicing Tips

It would be remiss of us not to give you information on juicing.

Juicing unlocks the goodness in fresh fruits and vegetables, drenching our bodies with nutrients. Although fibre content of produce is definitely important, sometimes it's better to drink our nutrition. Doing so enables the digestive system to work with a minimal amount of energy and effort.

There are many juicers on the market and likewise juicing books. Research for yourself the juicer that suits your needs. We use a Champion Juicer that has served us well. Keep in mind a juicer on a kitchen counter is likely to be used more often than one hidden away in the cupboard.

We recommend that you use organically grown produce whenever possible. If you cannot access organic produce, we suggest you peel the fruits and vegetables first or scrub them well with a fruit and vegetable wash concentrate, available at most health food stores.

The following recipes are basic juice combinations that we make. Once you get a working knowledge of juicing, you are on your way to creating flavorful nutritious drinks that suit your taste and individual needs.

Fresh Fruit Juice Recipes

Carrot and Apple Juice

- 6 carrots, tops removed
- 2 apples cored
- 1/2 inch piece of ginger

Juice all ingredients and serve immediately.

Serves 1 - 2

Carrot and Cabbage Juice

- 6 carrots, tops removed
- 6-8 inner cabbage leaves
- 1/2 inch piece of ginger

Juice all ingredients and serve immediately.

Serves 1 - 2

Cucumber and Apple Juice

- 1 cucumber
- 3 apples cored
- 1 tsp lemon peel

Juice all ingredients and serve immediately.

Serves 1 - 2

Cucumber and Celery Juice

- 1 cucumber
- 2 apples cored
- 2 celery stalks
- 1 large handful of parsley
- 2 sprigs of mint

Juice all ingredients and serve immediately.

Serves 1 - 2

Forest Fruit Slush

- 1 1/2 cups orange juice
- 1 Tbsp lime juice, freshly squeezed
- 3 cups frozen berries (blueberries, raspberries, blackberries)
- sweetener of choice if berries are tart

Pour orange juice, lime juice and berries into a blender. Process until smooth and slushy. Pour mixture into tall glasses. Add straws and serve garnished with berries.

Serves 2

Forest Fruit Smoothie

- 1 1/2 cups soy milk, regular or vanilla
- 1 banana sliced and frozen
- 3 cups frozen berries (blueberries, raspberries, blackberries)
- sweetener of choice if berries are tart

Pour soy milk into a blender. Add the banana and half the berries. Process until smooth. Add the remaining berries and sweetener if needed and process until smooth. Pour the mixture into tall glasses. Add straws and serve garnished with berries.

Serves 2

Herbal Iced Tea

Make refreshing iced tea to quench your thirst during those hot Okanagan summers.

- 4 herbal tea bags
- 2 cups boiled water
- 2 cups cooled water

Make an infusion of 4 tea bags and 2 cups boiling water. Steep for 5 minutes. Remove tea bags, stir in your sweetener of choice while the tea is still hot. Add 2 cups of cold water to the infusion and chill.

Try using lemon juice concentrate with a ratio of 1 Tbsp per cup of tea, instead of sweetener. For a slush type of drink, add chilled tea with ice cubes to a blender and blend until slushy. Some of our favorite teas are Passion, Wild Sweet Orange, Lemon Zinger, Wild Berry Zinger, Cranberry Apple Zinger, Tension Tamer and Berry Blossom.

Watermelon Cooler

- 4 cups cubed watermelon
- 4 Tbsp frozen concentrated lemonade or fresh lemon juice (to taste)
- fresh mint leaves

Wash the watermelon well. Cut off the rind and chop the watermelon into cubes, discarding the seeds. Put the watermelon and lemon in a blender and process until smooth. Place ice cubes in a tall glass. Add mint leaves. With a spoon, lightly bruise the leaves against the ice to release the mint flavor. Pour watermelon juice into glasses. Add a slice of lemon and a sprig of mint to garnish.

Serves 2

Frozen Berry Slush

- 4 cups cold water
- 1–335 ml can frozen concentrated lemonade
- 2 cups frozen raspberries or strawberries

Pour contents of lemon concentrate in a blender. Add 4 cups of cold water and 2 cups of frozen berries. Puree until berries are blended and mixture is slushy.

Serve in tall glasses with a wedge of freshly squeezed lemon.

Serves 10 - 12

Notes:

Salads

Salads

Avocado Salsa Salad

About Salad Dressings

Salad dressing usually requires a high oil ratio. To reduce the quantity of oil, use Instant Clear Gel. This is a modified cornstarch that thickens in a cold liquid.

To make a dressing thicker you can use various emulsifying agents. Some of our favourites are roasted garlic, avocados, tofu, dijon mustard, or mayonnaise.

The key to good dressing is a good oil. Try a variety of types including extra virgin olive, peanut, grape seed, toasted sesame and various nut oils.

To give your dressings a nice 'bite' use astringent agents such as fresh citrus juice (lemon, lime, orange, grapefruit), wine vinegars, balsamic vinegar, apple cider vinegar, rice vinegar, white vinegar, fruit vinegars, tamari, soy sauce, or Braggs aminos.

Use fresh herbs such as parsley, dill, tarragon, cilantro, fennel, chives, oregano, rosemary, savoury, thyme, basil.

Season with garlic, mustards, ginger, curry paste, capers, and dried vegetable seasonings (see Glossary).

To cut the acidity, use honey, maple syrup or organic cane sugar.

Apple Cider and Sour Cream Dressing

- 1/3 cup extra virgin olive oil
- 1/3 cup apple cider vinegar
- 1/4 cup soy sour cream
- 1 tsp dill
- 1 tsp organic cane sugar
- 1 tsp lemon and herb seasoning (see Glossary)

Whisk well.

Yields approximately 1 cup

Arizona Salad

This salad has a lovely presentation and tastes great.

- romaine lettuce for eight people
- 2 cups jicama julienned (see Cooking Terms)
- 1/2 medium red onion sliced
- 2 large avocadoes sliced
- 2 mangoes sliced
- 2 grapefruits sectioned
- 4 medium oranges sectioned
- 1/2 cup roasted almonds or pine nuts to garnish

Wash and dry romaine lettuce. Chop into pieces. Arrange on a platter. Cut pith from grapefruits and oranges. Remove sections from membrane (see Cooking Terms). Slice any thick sections and save the citrus juice. Set fruit aside. Marinate onion and avocado in the citrus juice. Prepare the jicama and mango. Decorate the platter of romaine with all the prepared fruit and vegetables.

Dressing for Arizona Salad

- 1/4 cup cider vinegar
- 1/4 cup lemon juice
- 1/4 cup extra virgin olive oil
- 1 Tbsp Garlic Plus seasoning (see Glossary)
- 1/4 tsp salt
- 1 tsp instant clear gel (see Glossary)
- 1 tsp dry sweetener of choice
- 1 clove grated garlic
- 1/2 tsp cumin

Add all ingredients to a blender and puree. Taste dressing and adjust seasonings. Drizzle over salad.

Serves 8

Arizona Salad

Asian Dressing

Add all ingredients to a blender and blend until smooth.

Yields 2 cups

- 1/2 cup sweet or red onion finely minced
- 3 Tbsp grated fresh ginger
- 4 cloves grated garlic
- 1 large orange, juiced
- 1 heaping Tbsp orange juice concentrate
- 3 Tbsp sodium reduced soy sauce
- 3 Tbsp toasted sesame oil
- 4 Tbsp grape seed or peanut oil
- 4 Tbsp rice wine vinegar
- 1/2 tsp instant clear gel

Balsamic Dijon Dressing

In a food processor or blender combine all ingredients except for the olive oil. Once mixed, continue to puree while slowly drizzling in the olive oil.
When finished blending, season further with sea salt and freshly ground pepper if desired.

Yields approximately 1 cup

- 1/3 cup balsamic vinegar
- 1/4-1/3 cup maple syrup
- 1 tsp Dijon mustard
- 2 tsp tamari, sodium reduced soy sauce or Braggs
- 1/4 tsp sea salt
- 1/8-1/4 tsp freshly ground black pepper
- 1/2 tsp dried oregano and/or rosemary
- 1/4 cup extra virgin olive oil

Basic Lemon Dressing

- 1/2 cup fresh lemon juice
- 1/4 cup extra virgin olive oil
- 1 clove minced garlic, 1 tsp roasted garlic or 1 tsp Garlic Plus seasoning
- 1 Tbsp honey
- 1/2 tsp instant clear gel (see Glossary)

Place all ingredients in a blender and blend until combined.

Variations: Blend in 1 cup of fresh parsley, cilantro or dill to make a fresh herb dressing.

Yields 1 1/2 cups

Cabbage Salad

- 1 small cabbage diced fine
- 1 1/2 cup diced celery
- 1 cup shredded carrot
- 1 cup crushed canned pineapple, drained (optional)
- 1/2 cup Tofu Mayonnaise (see recipe page 110)
- 3 Tbsp honey mustard
- salt to taste

Mix diced cabbage, carrot, celery and pineapple together in a large bowl.
Add salt, mayonnaise, and honey mustard combine well.
Chill before serving.

Serves 6

Caesar Salad

Romaine lettuce - well washed and dried. Break into 2 inch lengths.

If romaine is slightly limp, crisp it in a bowl of ice cold water for at least 30 minutes. Make a recipe for Caesar Salad Dressing
Pour dressing in the bottom of a large salad bowl. Add prepared lettuce. Toss.

You can use the traditional topping of croutons. Make them from a home made bread or an artisan bread. Serve with Red Pepper Aioli with Garlic Toast (see recipe page 115).

An alternative to croutons is toasted sunflower or pumpkin seeds; these add fibre and extra protein to the salad.

To make a chicken type Caesar salad, fry commercial vegetarian chicken strips until golden and add to salad.

Fried tofu cubes (see recipes page 204) are a nice addition to this salad; they also look like croutons.

Caesar Salad Dressing

- 1 bulb roasted garlic
- 1 Tbsp capers
- 1 Tbsp caper juice
- 1/4 cup lemon juice
- 1/4 tsp salt
- 1/2 cup extra virgin olive oil
- 1 1/2 tsp Dijon mustard
- 2 Tbsp soy mayonnaise
- 2 cloves fresh minced garlic
- 1/4 tsp cracked pepper
- 1/3 cup grated soy parmesan cheese

Place all ingredients into a blender except for the olive oil. While blending, add the oil in a steady stream.

Note: To roast garlic, slice bulb at top and place on a sheet of tin foil. Sprinkle olive oil and salt over the garlic. Close the tin foil around the garlic so it makes a little package. Bake at 375° F for 40 minutes. Cool and pop garlic out of skin. Mash while still warm.

Yields 1 1/2 cups

Crisp Oriental Salad
Try this lightly refreshing salad with a hearty lentil soup.

- 3 celery sticks
- 1 carrot
- 1 cucumber
- 1 Tbsp sodium reduced soy sauce
- 2 tsp white vinegar
- 1 tsp toasted sesame oil
- 1 clove grated garlic

You can add peeled and julienned broccoli stems or kohlrabi julienned to this salad as well.

Cut all the vegetables into julienned pieces 2 inches long (see Cooking Terms). Peel the cucumbers and scoop out seeds if not seedless. If you are not eating immediately, refrigerate. Meanwhile, mix the soy sauce, vinegar, sesame oil and garlic. Put all vegetables on a platter and drizzle with vinaigrette.

Serves 4 - 6

Cucumber Fennel Salad

Fennel blends well with fruits, especially apples in this crisp salad.

- 1 cucumber peeled, halved, seeded and diced
- 1 small fennel bulb trimmed and finely slivered
- 1 Granny Smith apple, cored, quartered then sliced
- 2 Tbsp toasted and chopped almonds, pecans or walnuts, for garnish
- 2 Tbsp dried cranberries

Vinaigrette for Cucumber Fennel Salad

- 2 Tbsp fresh orange juice
- 2 Tbsp oil (walnut, almond or olive)
- 1 Tbsp chopped parsley
- 1 Tbsp chopped fennel green
- 1 Tbsp chopped mint
- $1/8$ tsp paprika
- salt, ground pepper
- $1/2$ tsp dry sweetener of choice

Arrange cucumber, fennel, and apple on a serving platter. In a small bowl, whisk vinaigrette until blended. Pour over salad, garnish with toasted nuts and cranberries.

Serves 4 - 6

Dressing

- 1 Tbsp rice wine vinegar
- 1 Tbsp sodium reduced soy sauce
- 1 Tbsp toasted sesame oil
- 1 clove garlic, grated
- 1/2 tsp instant clear gel (optional)

Salad

- 2 cups edamame, steamed and shelled
- 1/2 cup green onion, diced
- 1/2 cup celery, diced
- 1/2 cup daicon radish, diced
- 1/2 cup red radish, diced
- 1 cup cucumber, diced
- 4 cups shredded Chinese cabbage
- 1/4 cup parsley or cilantro, minced

Edamame Salad

In a blender process dressing until clear gel is dissolved. Set aside.
Spread Chinese cabbage on a platter.
Top with edamame mixture. Drizzle with dressing and garnish with parsley or cilantro. Serve chilled.

Serves 4 - 6

Four Bean Salad

- 2 cups (19 oz) canned kidney beans, drained
- 2 cups (19 oz) canned garbanzo beans, drained
- 1 cup green beans cooked al dente
- 1 cup yellow beans cooked al dente
- 1/2 cup diced celery
- 1 small red onion sliced in rings
- 1/2 large green pepper cut in strips
- 1/2 large red pepper cut in strips
- 2/3 cup lemon juice
- 2/3 cup honey
- salt to taste
- dash of cayenne

Drain and rinse canned beans; add cooked beans, celery, onion and pepper strips in a large bowl.

Blend lemon juice, honey and salt.
Pour over vegetables, cover and marinate in refrigerator overnight or for at least 6 hours. Serve chilled.

Serves 6

French Dressing

- 1 cup water
- 1/3 cup lemon juice
- 2 1/2 Tbsp honey
- 2 tsp paprika
- 1 tsp celery salt
- 1/2 tsp dried Italian seasoning
- 1/3 tsp garlic powder
- 2 tsp onion powder
- 1/2 tsp salt
- pinch of cayenne
- 1 1/2 tsp instant clear gel (see Glossary)
- 1/3 cup extra virgin olive oil

Place all ingredients except olive oil in blender and blend briefly.
Add oil slowly and blend until smooth.
Refrigerate. Serve chilled.

Makes 2 cups

Grape and Broccoli Salad

The sweetness of grapes adds a new dimension to broccoli.

Salad

- 4 cups small broccoli florets
- 1 cup halved seedless green grapes
- 1 cup of halved seedless red grapes
- 1/2 cup finely sliced celery
- 1/4 cup sliced green onion
- 1 cup jicama and/or sliced apple
- 1/2 cup sliced and toasted almonds or pine nuts (save some for garnish)

Dressing

- 1/2 cup Tofu Mayonnaise (see recipe page 110)
- 1/4 cup soy sour cream
- 1 Tbsp white vinegar
- 2 Tbsp dry sweetener of choice
- 1/4 tsp pepper
- 1/8 tsp salt

Blanch the broccoli for approximately 30 seconds (see Glossary).
Immerse immediately in a cold water bath.
Drain well, removing excess moisture with a cotton cloth.

Combine the broccoli, grapes, celery, onions, jicama, apple, and nuts in a large bowl.

Toss the salad dressing with the broccoli mixture. Garnish with toasted nuts. Add salt and pepper to taste.

Yields approximately 5 servings

Greek Salad

- 6 Roma tomatoes cubed
- 1 green pepper cubed
- 1 long English cucumber cubed
- 1 small sweet onion or red onion cubed
- 1/2 cup crumbled soy feta cheese
- 12 Kalamata olives

Prepare vegetables. Combine in a large bowl. Add crumbled soy feta and olives. Drizzle with dressing.

Greek Salad Dressing

- 1/2 cup fresh lemon juice
- 2 Tbsp extra virgin olive oil
- 1/2 tsp dried garlic vegetable seasoning
- 1 tsp dried ground oregano
- 1 tsp dry sweetener of choice
- 1 tsp red wine vinegar
- 1 tsp instant clear gel (see Glossary)
- pinch of cayenne and salt

Add ingredients to a blender and process until smooth. Adjust seasonings. Pour dressing over salad.

Serves 6 - 8

Mediterranean Pasta Salad

A summer favourite.

- 4 cups cooked rotini noodles
- $1/4$ cup pitted olives
- $1/2$ cup peppers diced
- 1 Tbsp green onion chopped
- 1 cup grape tomatoes (save for garnish)

Mix first four ingredients together in a bowl.

- $1/4$ cup extra virgin olive oil
- $1/4$ cup organic cane sugar
- 3 Tbsp organic ketchup
- 3 Tbsp apple cider vinegar
- salt to taste
- dash of cayenne
- $1/2$ tsp paprika

Dressing for Mediterranean Pasta Salad

Whisk together ingredients for dressing and pour over pasta salad.
Add grape tomatoes just before serving.

Serves 6

Tabbouleh

Potato Salad

If you are a potato salad lover, this recipe is one of the best.

- 4 cups cooked, diced potatoes cooled
- 1/2 cup finely diced celery
- 1/2 cup grated carrots
- 1/4 cup peas steamed al dente
- 1/4 cup diced dill pickles
- 1/4 cup chopped green onions
- 1/4 cup sliced radishes
- 1 Tbsp pickle juice
- 3 Tbsp fresh chopped dill
- 4 Tbsp honey mustard
- 1/2-3/4 cup Tofu Mayonnaise (see recipe page 110), or favourite purchased mayonnaise
- 1 small tomato cut in wedges (optional)
- salt and/or dried vegetable seasonings (see Glossary)
- green lettuce leaves
- paprika

In a medium bowl, mix together potatoes, celery, carrots, peas, dill pickles, green onions and radishes.

Mix pickle juice, dill, mustard, mayonnaise, dried vegetable seasonings or salt to taste. Toss with potato mixture.

Line a large glass bowl with lettuce leaves and spoon potato salad into bowl. Garnish edges of bowl with tomato wedges and sprinkle with paprika.

Chill before serving.

Serves 6

South West Salad

You can serve this tasty colourful salad in a lettuce wrap.

- 3 Tbsp olive oil
- 1 Tbsp grated ginger
- 1 1/2 tsp crushed cumin seeds
- 1 tsp crushed mustard seeds
- 1/2 cup chopped red bell peppers
- 1 cup fresh or frozen kernel corn
- 1 cup jicama, diced
- 1/2 cup cucumber, diced
- 1 medium avocado, diced
- 1/2 cup radish, diced
- 1/2 cup toasted pumpkin seeds
- 1 cup fresh cilantro chopped
- 1/4 cup lime or lemon juice
- salt
- pinch of cayenne or black pepper

Heat oil in skillet over medium heat. Add ginger, cumin seeds, mustard seeds and sauté until fragrant (about 1 minute). Add the bell peppers and corn. Cook for about 4 minutes, stirring several times.

Cool mixture. Toss this mixture with remaining ingredients. Season to taste.

To add more protein to this salad, add black, kidney or pinto beans.

Serves 6 - 8

Spinach and Strawberry Salad

Salad

- spinach for six
- strawberries for six
- 1/4 cup slivered almonds

Tear young tender spinach into bite-sized pieces. Remove any long stems.
Slice strawberries into desired thickness.
Lightly toast almonds.

Dressing

- 1/4 cup dry sweetener of choice
- 1/4 cup extra virgin olive oil
- 1/4 cup raspberry vinegar
- 1/2 tsp vegan worcheshire sauce
- 1/2 tsp minced red onion
- 1/4 tsp paprika

Blend together ingredients.
For a nice pink dressing, puree several strawberries with the dressing.

Arrange spinach and strawberries on a platter. Drizzle with dressing. Garnish with toasted almonds.

Makes approximately 1 cup of dressing

Spinach Sun-Dried Tomato Salad
This is a divine salad.

- 6 handfuls of fresh spinach
- 1 cup grated carrot
- 1 red bell pepper julienned into 1 1/2 inch pieces
- 1/2 cup red onion, sliced
- 1/2 cup sun-dried tomato (oil packed, drained)
- 1/2 cup grated soy feta
- 1/2 cup roasted almonds or pine nuts

Wash and prepare spinach tearing leaves into bite-size pieces, removing tough stems. Spread leaves on a serving platter. Sprinkle with grated carrot, red pepper, red onion, sun-dried tomatoes, soy feta and roasted nuts.

Note: Soak onion in a mixture of 1 Tbsp lemon juice and 1/4 tsp sugar if it is pungent. Drain before adding to the salad. Drizzle with Balsamic Dijon Dressing (see recipe page 78).

Serves 6 - 8

Sui Choy Salad

- 1 large Chinese cabbage
- 5 green onions
- 3 Tbsp non-dairy butter
- 1/2 cup sesame seeds
- 1/2 cup slivered almonds
- 4 cups dried chow mein noodles (eggless variety)

Chop green onions and thinly slice cabbage. Chill.

Melt 3 Tbsp of non-dairy butter under the broiler.
Stir in sesame seeds, almonds and broken up noodles.
Lightly brown these, watching carefully, as they can easily burn.

Dressing for Sui Choy Salad

- 1/2 cup dry sweetener of choice
- 1/2 cup rice wine vinegar
- 2 tsp sodium reduced soy sauce
- 1/3 cup olive oil mixed with 1/3 cup water
- 1-2 tsp instant clear gel (see Glossary)

Add sugar, vinegar and soy sauce to a blender. Slowly add the olive oil and water mixture.

Add instant clear gel and blend to thicken dressing. Adjust seasonings.

Toss cabbage with dressing. Arrange on serving platter and then sprinkle noodle mixture on top.

Yields approximately 8 - 10 servings

Tabbouleh

This Middle Eastern salad is refreshing with the combination of mint, parsley and lemon.

- 1/2 cup couscous, bulgur wheat, or quinoa cooked according to package directions
- 2 Tbsp fresh lemon juice
- 1/4 cup extra virgin olive oil
- 1/4 tsp allspice
- 1/4 tsp cinnamon
- 3 cloves grated garlic
- 1/2 tsp salt
- 1 tsp organic cane sugar (optional)
- 1/2 cup fresh chopped mint
- 4 cups fresh chopped parsley
- 3 green onions, chopped
- 3 large tomatoes, seeded, chopped, liquid drained

Make a salad dressing with the lemon juice, olive oil, allspice, cinnamon, garlic, salt and sugar. Combine grain of choice, mint, parsley, onions, cucumber and tomato. Drizzle with dressing. Toss gently. Serve chilled.

Serves 6 - 8

Tangy Orange Dressing

- $1/2$ cup fresh orange juice or lemon juice
- 3 Tbsp frozen orange juice concentrate
- 2 Tbsp apple cider vinegar
- 2 cloves roasted garlic
- $1/2$ tsp salt
- dash of cayenne pepper
- $1/4$ cup extra virgin olive oil
- 1-2 Tbsp maple syrup
- 1 tsp instant clear gel (optional)

Place all ingredients in blender and blend until combined. If too thin, add instant clear gel and blend again.

Chill and serve.

Yields 1 cup

Waldorf Salad

Living in the Okanagan Valley with all the varieties of apples available, we had to include our version of this old favourite.

- 1 1/2 cups cubed tart Granny Smith or Spartan apples
- 1 1/2 cups cubed buttery Jona Gold or Honey Crisp apples
- 1 1/2 cups cubed crisp Gala or Ambrosia apples
- 1 cup diced center stalk of celery
- 1 1/2 cups seedless grapes, halved
- 1/2 cup chopped parsley
- 1/4 cup chopped mint (optional)
- 1 cup halved, roasted pecans
- 1 cup soy sour cream
- 1/4 cup freshly squeezed orange juice
- 2 Tbsp grated orange zest
- pinch of salt

Wash apples well, core and cube. Immerse cut apples in a lemon water bath to prevent browning (8 cups of cold water, 1 Tbsp lemon juice). Drain lemon water and pat apples dry. Add celery, grapes, parsley, mint and pecans (save some for garnish).

Mix sour cream, orange juice, orange zest and salt. Combine all ingredients. Serve immediately.

Servest 6 - 8

Watermelon Feta Salad
Our Greek friends gasp at this combination . . . but it tastes great.

- 4 pounds ripe red watermelon
- 1 small red onion
- 1/2 cup pitted Kalamata olives
- 1 cup soy feta cheese
- 1/4 cup extra virgin olive oil
- 2 limes or lemons, juiced
- 1 bunch fresh mint, chopped
- fresh ground pepper

Cut rind from watermelon and remove any seeds. Slice watermelon into one-inch bite-sized pieces. Arrange on a serving platter. Cut red onion in half moon slices and marinate in a lemon-sugar mixture for 10–15 minutes (see below).

Cut feta into small cubes and arrange over the watermelon. Slice olives and add to salad. In a blender, make a dressing with the lemon juice, olive oil and chopped fresh mint. Drizzle dressing over salad. Garnish with fresh mint leaves and freshly ground pepper.

Note: Soak onion in a mixture of 1 Tbsp lemon juice and 1/4 tsp sugar if it is too pungent. Drain before adding to salad.

Serves 4 - 6

Wilted Greens with Orange Curry Dressing

When greens are plentiful, use them in a wilted salad. Try this double boiler method for fun.

- 1 cup fresh squeezed orange juice
- 1 garlic clove, minced
- 1 tsp curry paste or powder
- pinch of salt
- 2 Tbsp chopped red onion or shallots
- 2 Tbsp extra virgin olive oil
- 2 Tbsp dried cranberries
- 2 Tbsp dried apricots, chopped
- 6 cups mixed greens, spinach or Swiss chard, stemmed and washed
- 1/2 cup almonds or pecans, roasted

Simmer orange juice in small saucepan over medium heat until slightly reduced. If dried fruit is very dry, re-hydrate in the juice (see Cooking Terms).

Combine garlic, curry, salt, onion or shallots, salt and olive oil with reduced orange juice in a stainless steel bowl large enough to toss the greens. Bring several cups of water to a simmer in a pot large enough for the bowl to rest on (double boiler). Heat dressing in bowl over double boiler.

Add the greens and dried fruit to the bowl and toss with dressing using tongs. Toss until wilted (about 1 minute). Transfer greens to a serving platter. Garnish with toasted nuts.

Note: When using a double boiler, use an oven mitt or towel to hold onto hot bowl.

Serves 4

Dips, Spreads & Sauces

Dips, Spreads & Sauces

Whole Wheat Sunflower Bread, Parsley Galet

Artichoke Spread

A delightful version with few calories.

- ¹/2 cup medium tofu, packed
- ¹/4 cup soy mayonnaise (see Glossary)
- 2-3 small to medium garlic cloves, roughly chopped (can be roasted)
- 1 Tbsp freshly squeezed lemon juice
- 2 tsp rice vinegar
- ¹/8 tsp sea salt
- fresh black pepper to taste
- 1 cup marinated artichoke hearts, drained and coarsely chopped
- ¹/2 cup roughly chopped fresh spinach, packed
- 3-4 Tbsp chopped fresh parsley
- 2¹/2 Tbsp soy or rice parmesan
- ¹/2 Tbsp soy or rice parmesan (for topping)

Preheat oven to 375° F.

In a food processor puree the tofu, soy mayonnaise, garlic, lemon juice, vinegar, sea salt, and black pepper until well blended, scraping down the sides a couple of times.

Add the artichoke hearts, spinach, parsley and 2¹/2 Tbsp soy or rice parmesan and process until chunky. Transfer the mixture to an oiled baking dish and sprinkle with the ¹/2 Tbsp soy or rice parmesan.

Bake for 20-25 minutes (the top should be golden brown in spots). Remove, let cool slightly and serve.

This can be made ahead of time and refrigerated until ready to bake and serve, but the cooking time will increase.
Serve on crostini, crackers or favourite fresh bread.

Yields approximately 2 cups

Avocado Salsa

Turn this salsa into a tasty salad by adding chopped romaine lettuce.

- 4 small avocados
- 2 beefsteak tomatoes (seeds removed)
- 1/2 red onion
- 2 green onions
- 2 cloves of garlic, minced
- 1/2 cucumber (remove tough skin)
- 1/2 cup yellow or red pepper
- 1 hot pepper, minced (optional)
- 1 tsp salt
- 2 tsp extra virgin olive oil
- 1 lemon, juiced
- 1 bunch of cilantro (approximately 1 cup)

Remove seeds from tomato and pit from avocado and cut into bite size pieces. Chop red onion, green onions, cucumber and peppers. Combine all ingredients, add minced garlic (hot pepper) salt, olive oil, lemon and chopped cilantro. Toss salsa and marinate for at least a half hour.

Yields approximately 6 cups

Basic Cream Sauce

The Basic Cream Sauce is a foundational sauce for many recipes throughout this cookbook.

- 1 cup raw cashews or blanched almonds
- 1 cups water
- 2 tsp unbleached white flour
- 1 tsp salt
- 1 Tbsp vegetarian chicken style soup base
- 1/2 tsp onion powder
- 1/2 tsp celery salt
- 1/4 cup grated soy cheese
- pinch of cayenne (optional-do not add if wanting a plain white sauce)
- 2 cups water

Place cashews or almonds into blender, add 1 cup water and blend until smooth and creamy. Add all remaining ingredients, except 2 cups of water, and continue blending.

In a saucepan bring the 2 cups of water to a boil. Add blended mixture to the boiling water and stir constantly while bringing to a second boil. Taste and adjust seasoning. Use in recipes that call for a cream sauce.

Yields approximately 4 cups

Chutney - Fresh Mint

This refreshing dip is great with samosas.

- 1/2 cup fresh mint leaves
- 1/2 cup fresh cilantro
- 3 green onions
- 1 tsp salt
- 1 tsp sugar
- 1/3 cup lemon juice
- 2 Tbsp water

Wash the mint and cilantro well, removing any coarse stems. Chop the onions. Put all ingredients into a blender and process until smooth. Use as a dip for samosas.
This can be stored in the refrigerator for up to one week. It also freezes well.

Yields approximately 1 1/2 cups

Chutney - Fresh Mango

A fresh, simple chutney you can prepare in minutes.

- 2 ripe mangos, chopped fine
- juice of 1 lime
- 3 Tbsp of finely chopped cilantro
- salt and pepper to taste.

Combine all ingredients together and chill.

Makes 1 cup

Creamy Chicken Gravy

This delicious gravy highlights any entrée where you use gravy.

- 2 cups water
- 1/2 cup raw cashews
- 1 Tbsp unbleached white flour
- 1 Tbsp chicken style soup base (see Glossary)
- 2 tsp onion powder or dried vegetable seasoning (see Glossary)
- 1/4 tsp celery salt
- salt to taste (optional)
- 1 Tbsp sodium reduced soy sauce

Place all ingredients in blender and blend until smooth and creamy.
Pour blended mixture into small saucepan. Stir constantly over medium heat until thickened.

Serve hot with your favourite entrees.

Variation: Substitute beef style seasoning to make a beef gravy.

Makes 2 1/2 cups

Curry Sauce

A savoury sauce, easy to make and wonderful over vegetables, grains, pasta, or fried tofu cubes.

- 1/4 cup olive oil
- 1/4 cup flour
- 1 Tbsp curry paste
- 1 tsp garam masala
- 1/2 cup tomato puree
- 2 cups vegetarian chicken broth (see Soup Making Tips page 126)
- 1 cup cashew cream (blend one cup of rinsed raw cashews with one cup of water till creamy and smooth)
- 1/4 cup chopped cilantro
- 2 tsp fresh squeezed lemon juice

Heat olive oil, stir in flour, curry paste and garam masala. Cook over medium heat for about 2 minutes. Add the tomato puree and chicken stock. Stir together and simmer for five minutes on medium low heat. Add cashew cream, cilantro and lemon juice and continue to simmer for 30 minutes, stirring to prevent scorching.

Note: You can substitute 1 cup of coconut milk for the cashew cream.

Tip: To make blending cashews easier, add 2 cups of cashews and 2 cups of water to your blender. Refrigerate or freeze remaining cup of cashew cream for future recipes.

Makes 3 cups

Genovese Pesto

This is our version of pesto – the flavourful emerald green sauce originating from Genoa, Italy.

- 1/2 bulb garlic, roasted
- 1 cup fresh parsley leaves packed
- 1 cup fresh basil leaves packed
- 2/3 cup extra virgin olive oil
- 1/4 cup pine nuts, lightly roasted
- 1/2 cup soy parmesan
- 2 tsp fresh lemon juice
- salt to taste

Cut the top from a bulb of garlic, drizzle with olive oil and bake wrapped in foil in a 375° F oven for 40 minutes. When cool enough to handle, squeeze half the cloves into a blender. Save the remaining cloves for future use.

Wash parsley and basil in cold water. Remove any tough stems. Chop coarsely and place in blender. Add roasted pine nuts, parmesan, and lemon juice. Puree ingredients until smooth. Add salt to taste.

Serve over pasta, steamed vegetables, as a topping for pizza, in grilled sandwiches or in pesto bundles (see recipe page 183).

Note: 3 cloves of fresh, coarsely chopped garlic can be used in place of roasted garlic. Pesto can be frozen. Omit the parmesan and add to recipe after thawing.

Makes 1 1/2 cups

Hummus

This Middle Eastern dip is easy to make, full of protein and it tastes good.

- 3 cloves minced garlic
- 19 oz. can of garbanzos, rinsed and drained
- 1/4 cup tahini
- 3 Tbsp lemon juice
- 1 Tbsp olive oil
- 1 Tbsp toasted sesame oil
- 1 tsp cumin
- 1/4 tsp salt

Blend ingredients until smooth. Serve with grilled pitas, vegetable sticks or in wraps.

Note: Peanut or almond butter may be substituted for tahini.

Yields approximately 2 cups

Light Veggie Gravy

If you have sensitivity to nuts, try this recipe made with a roux.

- 1/4 cup extra virgin olive oil
- 1/4 cup unbleached flour
- 1 tsp paprika
- 1 tsp vegetable seasoning (see Glossary)
- 3 cups vegetarian chicken or beef broth (see Soup Making Tips page 126)

Make a roux (see Cooking Terms) with olive oil and flour. Cook on medium heat for several minutes. Add paprika and seasoning. Whisk stock in slowly to prevent lumps. Reduce heat to medium low and cook until sauce thickens. Turn heat to low and reduce (see Cooking Terms) gravy for 15-20 minutes. Adjust seasoning. Serve where you would gravy.

Makes 3 cups

Mayonnaise - Tofu

Easy to make and much more cost effective than commercial.

- 1-349g (12.3 oz) firm Silken tofu
- 1 Tbsp fresh squeezed lemon
- 1 Tbsp apple cider vinegar
- 1 Tbsp organic cane sugar
- 1/2 tsp onion powder
- 3/4 tsp salt
- 2 Tbsp extra virgin olive oil
- 1 tsp Dijon mustard
- 1 tsp dried vegetable seasoning

In a blender or food processor, process all ingredients until smooth.
Pour into a jar and refrigerate. Will last up to five days refrigerated.

Makes 1 1/2 cups

Mayonnaise - Almond

A tasty alternative spread for the soy sensitive.

- 1 cup blanched almonds
- 3/4 cup rice or almond milk
- 4 tsp flour
- 2 tsp nutritional yeast
- 1 tsp garlic powder
- 1 tsp salt
- 3/4 cup extra virgin olive oil
- 6 tsp lemon juice
- 1 tsp dried basil
- 1 tsp dried oregano
- 1/3 cup water

Blend almonds, milk, flour and nutritional yeast until almonds are smooth and creamy.

Add remaining ingredients to blended almonds.

Blend ingredients well. Refrigerate in a glass jar.

Yields 2 cups

Parsley Galet

Use the best non-dairy butter you can find for this spread. It's delicious served on fresh bread or steamed vegetables.

- 2 cups non-dairy butter
- 2 Tbsp tomato paste
- zest of 1 lemon, finely minced
- 2 cups of minced parsley (remove tough stems)

Thoroughly combine all of the ingredients except for the parsley. Work fairly quickly as the butter liquefies at room temperature. On a piece of plastic wrap sprinkle the parsley into a rectangular shape. The layer can be as long as one desires; just make sure that there are no large spaces where the spread will soak through. Place the mixture down the center of the parsley.

Fold both lengths of the plastic together and form a tube.
Shape the tube lightly and twist the ends of the plastic wrap.
Place on a flat surface and chill in the freezer. Once solid, cut into thin slices and serve with rolls or over vegetables.

Refrigerate unused spread.

Yields approximately a 10 inch tube

Tzatziki, Spanakopita

Peanut Butter Dipping Sauce

This dipping sauce has a nice curry taste. Use it for rice paper or lettuce wraps.

- 1/4 cup smooth peanut butter
- 2 cloves garlic minced
- 1 Tbsp ginger minced
- 2 Tbsp honey
- 1/4 cup minced cilantro
- 1 Tbsp lime juice
- 1 Tbsp toasted sesame oil
- 1 tsp curry paste
- 1/4 cup sodium reduced soy sauce
- 2 Tbsp rice wine vinegar

Mix all ingredients in a blender.
If mixture thickens too much, add a small amount of water.

Note: Almond butter can be used in place of peanut butter.

Yields approximately 1 cup

Pear Cream

Once you've tasted Pear Cream, you'll try to find many ways to use it. Drizzle over hot fruit crisps, hot cereal, fruit salad.

- 1/2 cup raw cashews or blanched almonds, rinsed
- 1/4 tsp salt
- 1 tsp vanilla
- 1 tsp honey (optional)
- 1-28 oz can of pears
- 1 cup pear juice

Place nuts in blender. Add some pear juice and blend until very smooth.
Add remaining ingredients to blender and continue blending until you have a thick, smooth consistency. Add more juice if necessary. Chill well.

Makes 4 cups

Red Bell Pepper Purée

This intensely flavoured puree is splendid. Serve a spoonful in cream soups, in grilled sandwiches, over pasta, or on pizza.

- 5 large red bell peppers
- extra virgin olive oil
- fresh lemon
- salt
- sugar (optional)

Seed peppers and cut into large pieces. Arrange on baking pan and drizzle with olive oil. Bake at 350° F for 30 minutes or until tender. You can also cook the peppers in a covered skillet with olive oil over low heat until tender. Puree the peppers in a blender or food processor. Add enough olive oil to make a smooth paste, add the juice of half a squeezed lemon, a pinch of salt and sugar if the puree is too tart.

Yields 1/2 cup

Red Pepper Aioli

Use this aioli as a spread for grilled sandwiches on garlic toast, or use as a dipping sauce for yam fries.

- 2 tsp roasted garlic
- 1/2 cup roasted bell peppers, skinned, drained and patted dry
- 1/3 cup soy mayonnaise
- 2 Tbsp extra virgin olive oil
- salt and freshly ground black pepper
- 1 tsp dried roasted garlic, red peppers seasoning

Line a baking sheet with foil. Halve and seed peppers. Place face side down on baking sheet. Cut top from garlic and drizzle with olive oil. Make a foil packet and wrap garlic. Bake both garlic and peppers in 400° F oven for 30-40 minutes until pepper skin begins to blacken and blister. Cool peppers in a covered bowl. Peel when cool. Squeeze garlic from bulb. Refrigerate unused portion.

Add the roasted garlic, peppers, mayonnaise and olive oil to a blender and process until smooth. Season with salt, pepper and roasted garlic and peppers seasoning.

Cover and refrigerate.

Makes 1 cup

Tapenade

Olives and sun-dried tomatoes are rich concentrated flavours.
If you love olives this spread is for you.

- 1 cup Kalamata olives, pitted
- 2 cloves garlic grated
- 1/4 cup capers
- 1/4 cup extra virgin olive oil
- 1 Tbsp balsamic vinegar
- 3 Tbsp sun-dried tomatoes packed in oil
- 1/2 cup minced parsley (save some for garnish)

Place all ingredients into blender or food processor and blend to a coarse consistency, or chop ingredients very fine. Serve in condiment bowl, garnished with parsley. Serve crackers or crostini on the side. Try tossing it with hot pasta, or serve a spoonful in a small endive leaf as an appetizer.

Yields approximately 1 cup

Tofu Cottage Cheese

Served on baked potatoes, in a lasagne or any time you would use a dairy cottage cheese.

- 1-454 g pkg medium tofu, rinsed and drained overnight
- 1/4 tsp garlic powder
- 1/4 tsp onion powder
- 1/2 tsp lemon juice
- 1 tsp salt
- 1/2 cup raw cashews
- 1/4 cup pickle juice or water (reduce salt if using pickle juice)
- 1/3 cup dill minced (optional)

Crumble tofu into a small bowl
Place remaining ingredients in blender and blend until smooth, adding just enough pickle juice to form a creamy sauce.
Pour blended sauce over crumbled tofu and mix well. Chill before serving.

Note: To drain tofu overnight, wrap in a towel and place in a colander. Refrigerate.

Makes 3 cups

Tofu Preparation Tips

Marinated tofu is a very versatile food staple to have in your refrigerator. Add it to stir-fried vegetables, fried rice or serve it with a sauce over grains or noodles.

When marinating medium tofu, first drain the packing liquid. Rinse, then return the tofu block to its packaging that has been lined with cheese cloth or paper towel. Refrigerate overnight. The cloth will absorb moisture from the tofu. Should you forget to drain tofu overnight, you can follow the same process of removing it from its packaging and rinsing. For this method, cut the block in thirds. Line a colander with a dishcloth. Place the tofu in the colander. Lay another cloth on top and add weight such as canned goods. Let it press for at least 30 minutes. Cut the pieces into 1/2 inch thickness and add to the marinade. These amounts are for a 454 g package of tofu.

Tip: Keep aseptic packaged silken tofu in your pantry for emergencies. It doesn't require refrigeration, and has a long shelf life.

Tofu Marinade Recipes

Mix marinade ingredients together in an oven-proof baking dish. Arrange the tofu on the marinade. The tofu won't be covered by the marinade. You will have to turn the tofu during the marinating process to cover both sides. The longer you leave the tofu in the marinade, the more flavourful it will be. We suggest overnight.

Bake in the ovenproof dish at 400° F for 30-40 minutes or fry stovetop on medium heat about 10 minutes on each side.

Asian
- 1 Tbsp sodium reduced soy sauce
- 1 Tbsp blackbean, Hoisin sauce or blackbean garlic paste
- 1 Tbsp grated ginger
- 1 tsp Five-Spice powder (optional)
- 2 Tbsp toasted sesame oil
- 1/3 cup grape seed or peanut oil

Indian
- 1 Tbsp curry paste or powder
- 1 tsp garam masala
- 1/2 tsp ground cumin seeds crushed
- 1/2 tsp ground coriander seeds, crushed
- 1/3 cup grape seed or peanut oil

Mexican
- 1 Tbsp chilli powder
- 1 tsp canned chipotle pepper minced
- 1 tsp smoked paprika
- 1/2 tsp ground cumin
- 1/3 cup grape seed or peanut oil

Tzatziki

Serve this refreshing dip with Spanakopitas and Greek salad.

- 1 long English cucumber
- 1 1/2 cups plain soy sour cream
- 2 tsp white vinegar
- 4 cloves of roasted and mashed garlic
- 1 Tbsp fresh dill chopped
- salt and pepper to taste

Grate cucumber and parsley. Using a cotton cloth gently squeeze out excess juice. Mix sour cream, vinegar, mashed garlic and dill. Add seasonings and cucumber. Garnish with fresh dill. Refrigerate.

Yields approximately 2 1/2 cups

Vegan Hollandaise Sauce

Serve this creamy Hollandaise drizzled over Tofu Benedict or Steamed Vegetables.

- 1-150 g package dessert tofu
- 1/4 tsp Dijon mustard
- 1 Tbsp lemon juice
- dash of paprika (hot)
- 1/2 cup non-dairy butter, melted
- 1 cup tofu milk (or milk of choice)
- 1 Tbsp soy mayonnaise
- 1 tsp cornstarch
- 1/4 tsp turmeric for colour
- 1 Tbsp red or white wine vinegar
- 1/2 tsp dried tarragon, chopped
- 1 tsp organic cane sugar (or to taste)

Put everything in blender except tarragon and vinegar. Blend. Put sauce in sauce pan over medium heat and bring to a low boil. Stir to prevent scorching. Remove from heat, add tarragon and red wine vinegar. Add sweetener if needed.

Yields 2 cups

Velvet Cheese Spread

This creamy spreadable cheese is tasty on celery sticks, served on crackers or as a spread for sandwiches.

- $1/4$ cup water
- 1 Tbsp unflavoured gelatin (see Glossary)
- $3/4$ cup boiling water
- 1 cup raw cashews
- $1 1/2$ tsp salt
- 1 tsp garlic plus (see Glossary)
- 1 Tbsp lemon juice
- 2 Tbsp chopped red pepper
- $2/3$ cup soy cheddar cheese (optional)

Place gelatin and $1/4$ cup water in the blender and let soak for 5 minutes.

Pour boiling water over soaked gelatin and blend briefly to dissolve. Allow mixture to cool slightly.

Add cashews and blend until very smooth.

Add remaining ingredients and continue to blend until mixture is creamy.

Pour mixture into an oiled container and let cool. Cover and refrigerate overnight.

Makes 3 cups

Vietnamese Dipping Sauce

This sauce is lighter than the peanut sauce. Another good choice for your rice or lettuce wraps.

- 1/2 cup toasted sesame oil
- 1 cup sodium reduced soy sauce
- 1/2 cup rice vinegar
- 1 tsp liquid honey
- 2 Tbsp grated ginger
- 2 Tbsp Thai sweet chilli sauce

Whisk all ingredients until well combined.

Yields approximately 2 cups

Soups

Soups

Minestrone Soup

Introduction to Soup Making

Soup for an evening meal is light and nourishing. Its liquid nature makes soup more easily digestible than drier, heavier foods.

Here are a few tips for soup making.

Always use high quality ingredients. "Fridge Clean" soup won't miraculously resurrect those old leftovers into a good soup.

Cruciferous vegetables (members of the cabbage family) such as cabbage, brussels sprouts, broccoli and cauliflower can overwhelm a soup if boiled vigorously. Simmer these soups.

Save florettes from broccoli and cauliflower, tips of asparagus, and fresh peas. Blanch and add to soups at the end of cooking time for added texture. Most people will not take time to make a complicated stock. We have given you a simple recipe for a roasted vegetable stock.

To save time, purchase a good quality soup base mix. When a recipe calls for broth, make it according to your soup base directions.

Sauté your vegetables to release their natural sugars. It adds sweetness to the soup. Some examples are: carrots, onions, celery, cabbage, yams, sweet potatoes.

When using pungent spices such as chili, curry, and cumin, add them to the sautéed vegetables to release their flavours prior to adding the stock. When adding dry herbs such as thyme, dill, oregano, basil, and savoury, add to the soup after it has come to a full boil and soup is simmering.

When adding fresh herbs such as parsley, cilantro, and dill, add to the soup about ten minutes prior to serving.

Our cream soups are made with cashew cream. Always blend the cashews smooth and creamy. If the soup is thin, add flour to the cashew cream. Stir the soup continuously and pour the cream in a steady stream. Simmer soup after the cream has been added.

At the end of cooking time, always taste your soup and adjust seasonings. If your soup seems to be missing that little bit of something, try adding 1 Tbsp of fresh lemon juice or balsamic, red or white wine vinegar, depending on the soup.

Black Bean Soup

You'll savour the subtle smokiness and spice in this creamy soup.

- 1 Tbsp olive oil
- 1 medium onion, diced fine
- 1 clove of garlic, diced fine
- 1 Tbsp cumin
- 1 tsp smoked paprika
- 1 Tbsp canned chopped chipotle pepper (remove seeds for less heat)
- 1/2 cup tomato salsa
- 2 cups vegetarian beef broth (see Soup Making Tips)
- 1-28 oz can of diced plum tomatoes
- 2 cups tomato or V8 juice
- 1-19 oz can of black beans, drained and rinsed
- 1/4 cup minced fresh cilantro
- 1 cup cashews
- 1 cup water

Sauté onion and garlic in olive oil, using a medium sized soup pot. Add cumin, paprika and chipotle pepper. Sauté for several minutes. Add salsa, soup broth, tomato juice and tomatoes. Bring to a rolling boil. Reduce heat.

Using a potato masher or food processor, mash most of the black beans into a paste leaving just a few as broken beans. Add beans to simmering broth along with the cilantro. Simmer for about 30 minutes.

Blend cashews in blender with water until creamy and smooth. (You will probably only need 1 cup of cashew cream for this recipe. Refrigerate or freeze remaining cup for another recipe.)

Drizzle cashew cream into soup, stirring constantly.

Simmer for another 1/2 hour, stirring to prevent scorching. Taste and adjust seasonings. Garnish with minced cilantro.

Serves 6

Chicken Noodle Soup

Soup to make you feel better.

- 2 tsp olive oil
- 1/2 cup diced onion
- 1/2 cup diced celery
- 1/2 cup grated carrot
- 1/2 tsp celery salt
- pinch of cayenne
- 6 cups vegetarian chicken broth (see Soup Making Tips)
- 1/2 cup fried veggie chicken strips (see Glossary)
- 3 cups cooked, rinsed whole wheat spaghetti (broken into 1 inch lengths)
- parsley, chopped

Sauté onion, celery and carrot until onion is translucent.
Add chicken broth, celery salt and cayenne .
Bring stock to a boiling point.
Reduce heat then add cooked veggie chicken and cooked spaghetti noodles.
Simmer for 10 minutes.
Garnish with fresh parsley.

Serves 6

Corn Chowder

Creamy goodness – especially with freshly picked corn.

- 1 Tbsp olive oil
- $1/2$ cup diced onion
- $1/2$ cup diced celery
- $1/2$ cup diced carrot
- $1/2$ cup diced red pepper
- 4 cups fresh or frozen kernel corn
- $1 1/2$ cups peeled cubed potatoes
- $1/4$ cup minced parsley, fresh or dried
- 1 Tbsp roasted garlic and red peppers seasoning (see Glossary)
- 1 bay leaf
- 6 cups vegetarian chicken broth (see Soup Making Tips)
- 1 cup raw cashews
- 1 cup water
- $1/2$ cup fresh parsley, chopped for garnish

Sauté onion, celery, carrot and red pepper until onion is translucent.
Add corn, potatoes and seasonings.
Add chicken broth, and bring to a boil.
Simmer for 30 minutes or until potatoes and corn are cooked.
Blend cashews and water until smooth and creamy.
Slowly add to soup, stirring constantly.
Simmer for 10-15 minutes.
Adjust seasonings and remove bay leaf.
Serve garnished with fresh parsley or smoked paprika.

Serves 6

Cream of Asparagus Soup

- 4 cups vegetarian chicken broth (see Soup Making Tips)
- 1 small onion, chopped
- 2 ribs celery, chopped
- 1 pound asparagus tips removed and saved for later
- 1 bay leaf
- 1 Tbsp olive oil
- 1/2 cup minced onion
- 1/2 cup chopped carrot
- 1/2cup chopped celery
- 1 tsp celery salt
- 1/4 tsp cayenne pepper
- 1 tsp dried vegetable seasoning (see Glossary)
- 1 cup water
- 1 cup cashews
- 4 Tbsp flour
- 1 Tbsp fresh lemon juice
- 1/2 cup minced parsley (save some for garnish)

Put stock, onion, celery, asparagus stems (tough ends and any hard skin removed), and bay leaf into a soup pot. Bring to a full boil and cook until vegetables are soft. Cool mixture and remove bay leaf.

Puree in blender until smooth. Transfer back to soup pot.

Cut asparagus tips into bite-sized pieces. Steam for 30 seconds, then drop them into a cold water bath until cooled. Drain.

Sauté onion, carrot, celery, celery salt, cayenne and dried vegetable seasoning until onion is translucent. Add to puree mixture.
Blend cashews, flour and water until smooth and creamy.
Drizzle cashew cream into soup, stirring constantly.
Simmer until soup thickens.
Add steamed asparagus tips, parsley and fresh lemon juice.
Simmer for 5 minutes. Taste and adjust seasonings.
Serve garnished with parsley.

Serves 4 - 6

Cream of Broccoli and Spinach Soup

To add colour to this soup, we've added fresh spinach and parsley. Try fresh lovage - it tastes great as well.

- 1 Tbsp olive oil
- 1 cup diced onion
- 1 cup diced celery
- 2 cloves garlic, minced
- 4 cups broccoli stalks, peeled and chopped (save florettes)
- 6 cups vegetarian chicken broth (see Soup Making Tips)
- 2 cups chopped fresh spinach
- 2 Tbsp dried parsley (or 1/2 cup fresh chopped)
- 1 tsp celery salt
- 1 tsp dried vegetable seasoning (see Glossary)
- 1 bay leaf
- 3 cups broccoli florettes
- 1 cup raw cashews
- 1 cup water
- 2 Tbsp flour
- 1/4 cup minced fresh parsley
- 1 Tbsp fresh lemon juice

Heat oil in a large soup pot. Sauté onion, celery, garlic, and chopped broccoli stalks until onion is translucent. Add broth, spinach, parsley, celery salt, vegetable seasoning and bay leaf. Bring mixture to a low boil. Reduce heat. Remove bay leaf and puree soup with a hand held blender or table top blender. Careful blending hot liquid! You may want to cool the soup before putting it in a blender.

Break saved broccoli florettes into bite-sized pieces. Blanch for 3 minutes. Drop into cold water bath until cooled. Drain.
Blend cashews, water and flour until smooth and creamy. Add to soup, stirring constantly over medium low heat. Simmer soup until cashew cream thickens. Add blanched broccoli and lemon. Taste and adjust seasonings. Garnish with parsley prior to serving.

Serves 6 - 8

Cream of Cauliflower Soup
Creamy with sweet little peas throughout – Yum!

- 1 Tbsp olive oil
- 1 cup diced onion
- 1 cup diced celery
- 1 cup diced carrot
- 1 1/2 cups chopped fresh cauliflower (save some florettes for garnish)
- 2 cups diced peeled potatoes
- 6 cups vegetarian chicken broth (see Soup Making Tips)
- 1 bay leaf
- 2 Tbsp dried parsley
- 1 tsp celery salt
- 1 tsp dried vegetable seasoning (see Glossary)
- 1 cup frozen or fresh peas
- 1/2 cup minced fresh parsley
- 1 cup raw cashews
- 1 cup water
- 2 Tbsp flour
- fresh parsley for garnish

Heat oil in large soup pot. Add onion, celery carrot and cauliflower. Sauté until onion is translucent. Add broth, potatoes and bay leaf. Simmer on medium heat until potatoes and cauliflower are cooked. Add parsley, celery salt and dried vegetable seasoning.

Break saved cauliflower florettes into bite size pieces. Blanch for 3 minutes.
Drop into a cold water bath until cooled. Drain.
Blend cashews, water and flour until smooth and creamy. Add to soup, stirring constantly on medium-low heat. Simmer soup until cashew cream thickens. Remove bay leaf. Taste, and adjust seasonings. Add peas, parsley, and blanched florettes. Simmer 5 minutes.

Serve garnished with chopped parsley.

Serves 6 - 8

Cucumber Soup

One would never know that cucumbers are the key ingredient to this creamy soup. Serve when field cucumbers are plentiful.

- 1 cup chopped onion
- 1/2 cup finely chopped celery
- 1 cup finely chopped carrot
- 1 Tbsp olive oil
- 1/4 cup flour
- 4 cups vegetarian chicken broth
- 2 bay leaves
- 3 cups peeled finely chopped potatoes
- 5 medium field cucumbers, peeled, deseeded, diced
- 1 tsp dried dill
- 1 Tbsp dried vegetable seasoning
- 1 cup cooked rice (optional)
- 1/2 cup raw cashews
- 2/3 cup water
- 2 Tbsp freshly squeezed lemon juice
- 1/2 cup minced fresh parsley

Sauté onion, celery and carrot in olive oil on medium heat until onion is translucent. Add flour and stir to coat vegetables. Sauté for several minutes. Add chicken broth, bay leaves and potatoes.

Turn heat to high and boil potatoes until al dente. Reduce heat to medium. Add cucumbers and simmer for about 10 minutes. Remove bay leaves. Pour half the mixture in a blender and puree until smooth. Be careful blending hot liquid. You may want to quick chill before blending.

Pour pureed mixture into soup. Add dill, vegetable seasoning and rice. Reduce heat and simmer for 20 minutes. Blend cashews and water until smooth and creamy. Add to soup along with lemon juice and parsley. Save a few tablespoons of parsley for garnish. Simmer for 10 minutes. Garnish and serve warm.

Serves 8

Roasted Red Pepper Soup, Empanadas

Curried Carrot Soup

A velvety soup with a nice blend of spices.

- 2 Tbsp olive oil
- 1 medium onion, chopped
- 2 ribs celery, chopped
- 4 cups peeled and chopped carrots
- 3 cloves minced garlic
- 2 Tbsp fresh ginger grated
- 1 Tbsp curry paste or powder
- 1 tsp garam masala
- 1 Tbsp flour
- 6 cups vegetarian chicken broth (see Soup Making Tips)
- 1-14 oz (398 ml) can coconut milk or 1 1/2 cups cashew cream (see recipe page 104)
- 1/2 cup minced cilantro (save some for garnish)
- 1 Tbsp freshly squeezed lemon

To speed the process, put onion, celery and carrot in a food processor and chop fine. Heat olive oil in a soup pot. Add onion, celery and carrot. Sauté until carrot starts to change colour. Add garlic, ginger, curry and garam masala. Sauté for several minutes until seasonings release their flavours.

Add flour, cook for about 2 minutes longer. Transfer sautéed mixture to a blender. This may have to be done in several batches. Puree with enough stock to blend until smooth. Return puree to the soup pot on medium heat. Add coconut milk or cashew cream. Bring to a boil. Reduce heat. Add cilantro, saving some for garnish. Add lemon. Taste and adjust seasonings.

Serves 8

Fresh Pea Soup with Mint

What a wonderful way to eat garden fresh peas.

- 3 Tbsp olive oil
- 2 cups diced sweet onion
- 3 cloves garlic, minced
- 3 cups peas (fresh or frozen)
- 4 cups fresh spinach (stems removed)
- 4 cups vegetarian chicken broth (see Soup Making Tips)
- 1/2 cup chopped fresh mint leaves
- 1 Tbsp fresh lime juice
- minced fresh parsley or soy sour cream to garnish

Heat oil over medium heat.
Sauté onion and garlic until onion is translucent.
Stir in spinach. Sauté until spinach wilts slightly.
Add broth and peas; simmer for several minutes until peas turn bright green.
Careful not to overcook!

Remove from heat and puree soup with mint until smooth and creamy. You may have to do this in batches.

Return soup to the pot and season with lime juice and salt. Serve hot.
Garnish with minced fresh parsley and a dollop of soy sour cream.

Serves 6

Garden Vegetable Soup

Add tomato paste or curry paste to individual servings for a taste variation.

- 1 cup diced carrots
- 1/2 cup diced onion
- 1 clove garlic, minced
- 3 cups chopped cabbage
- 2 ribs diced celery
- 6 cups vegetarian chicken broth (see Soup Making Tips)
- 1 cup green beans cut into 2 inch pieces (fresh or frozen)
- 1 cup kernel corn (fresh or frozen)
- 1 cup peeled cubed potatoes
- 1 bay leaf
- 1 tsp dried oregano
- 2 tsp dried vegetable seasoning (see Glossary)
- 1/2 cup fresh parsley chopped

Sauté carrots, onion, garlic, cabbage and celery until soft.

Add chicken broth and bring to a boil.

Add green beans, corn, potatoes and seasonings.
Reduce heat and simmer until vegetables are tender 25-35 minutes.

Taste and adjust seasonings. Garnish with parsley.

Serves 8

Italian Soup

This hearty soup is a meal in itself.

- 1/2 minced onion
- 1 clove minced garlic
- 28 oz can diced tomatoes
- 1 cup tomato or V8 juice
- 1 Tbsp tomato paste
- 5 cups vegetarian chicken or beef broth (see Soup Making Tips)
- 1 1/2 cups fresh or frozen cut green beans
- 1 1/2 cups fresh or frozen kernel corn
- 2 cups chopped spinach
- 1 tsp oregano dried
- 1 tsp basil dried
- 1 bay leaf
- 1 cup romano or pinto beans
- 1/2 cup chopped parsley
- 1/2 cup grated soy parmesan
- 2 cups cooked whole wheat pasta (any shape)
- 1 Tbsp balsamic vinegar
- 1/2 cup grated soy parmesan

Sauté onion and garlic until golden. Add tomatoes, tomato juice, tomato paste, soup broth, green beans, corn and spinach.

Bring to a low boil. Reduce heat then add seasonings and beans.
Simmer over medium heat for 40-60 minutes. Remove bay leaf.

Add pasta, parsley and balsamic vinegar prior to serving, and garnish with parmesan cheese.

Serves 8

Lentil Soup

This recipe is a favourite with the guests.

- 3 cups green lentils (masoor dal)
- 1 bay leaf
- 1 garlic clove, mashed
- 1 medium onion, minced
- 2 ribs diced celery
- 2 large diced carrots
- 1 Tbsp garam masala
- 1 Tbsp curry paste
- 1-28 oz can diced tomatoes
- 2 cups tomato or V8 juice
- 4 cups vegetarian beef broth (see Soup Making Tips)
- 2 cups peeled cubed potatoes or 2 cups cooked basmati rice
- 1/2 cup chopped cilantro
- 1/2 cup chopped parsley

In a pot, using cold water, soak 3 cups green lentils (masoor dal) for a minimum of 2 hours.

Add 1 bay leaf, 1 garlic clove mashed and enough water to cover the lentils.
Then bring to a boil. Cook for 40-45 minutes.

In a separate soup pot sauté the onion, celery, carrots, garam masala and curry paste until soft.

To the sautéed mixture add diced tomatoes, tomato or V8 juice, vegetarian beef broth, potatoes, cilantro and parsley.

Remove bay leaf and garlic from lentils. Drain lentils. Add to the soup pot with sautéed vegetables, tomatoes, juice, broth, potatoes, and cilantro.
Simmer for approximately 40 minutes or until potatoes are tender.

Taste and adjust seasonings. Garnish with chopped parsley.

Serves 8

Fresh Pea Soup, Pesto Bundles

Minestrone Soup

This soup is a lighter version of the Italian soup.

- 2 Tbsp olive oil
- 2 cups chopped onion
- 3 medium cloves garlic
- 1 stalk celery, diced
- 2 cups sliced cabbage
- 2 cups diced zucchini
- 1 medium bell pepper, diced
- 1 tsp dried oregano
- 1 tsp dried basil
- 6 cups vegetarian chicken broth (see Soup Making Tips)
- 2 medium-size seeded and diced tomatoes or 1 cup diced canned tomatoes
- 2 cups cooked kidney, navy or pinto beans
- 2 cups cooked, whole wheat pasta (any shape)
- 1/2 cup fresh minced parsley
- 1/2 cup parmesan cheese

Heat olive oil; sauté onion, garlic, celery, and cabbage over medium heat for about 8 minutes.

Add zucchini, red pepper, oregano, basil, soup broth, tomatoes and kidney beans. Simmer until soup comes together (about 30 minutes).

Taste and adjust seasonings. Add the cooked pasta and simmer for about 5 minutes.

Serve topped with parmesan and parsley.

Serves 6 - 8

Onion Soup

You'll love the richness of this soup.

- 1 Tbsp olive oil
- 4 medium onions
- 3 cloves minced garlic
- 2 tsp paprika
- 1 tsp freshly ground pepper or $1/2$ tsp cayenne pepper
- 2 tsp dried vegetable seasoning (see Glossary)
- 1 tsp dried oregano
- 1 Tbsp tomato paste
- 1 cup tomato or V8 juice
- 2 Tbsp balsamic vinegar or red wine vinegar
- 1 bay leaf
- 6 cups vegetarian beef stock (see Soup Making Tips)

Heat olive oil in a soup pot. Peel onion, cut in half lengthwise, then slice thinly.
Sauté onions on medium-low heat with garlic and paprika. Take time to get the onions to a caramel colour without burning (about 20 minutes).

Add ground pepper, vegetable seasoning, oregano, tomato paste, tomato juice, balsamic vinegar, bay leaf and vegetarian beef broth. Simmer for 30-40 minutes. Taste. Adjust seasonings. Remove bay leaf.

Make cheese toast with soy mozzarella and Parmesan cheese.
Cut into bite-sized pieces.
Ladle soup into bowls and top with the cheese toast.

Serves 4

Roasted Red Pepper Soup

The smoked paprika and chipotle peppers give this soup a little bit of kick.

- 2 red bell peppers
- 2 green peppers
- 2 large garlic bulbs
- 4 cups vegetarian chicken soup broth (see Soup Making Tips)
- 2 cups diced tomato canned or fresh
- 1 can condensed tomato soup
- 1 Tbsp balsamic vinegar
- 1 Tbsp organic cane sugar
- 1 tsp smoked paprika
- 1 tsp canned or powdered chipotle pepper
- 2 cups fresh or frozen beans French cut
- 1 cup cooked brown rice
- 1/2 cup minced parsley

Line a baking sheet with foil.
Halve and seed peppers. Place face side down on baking sheet.
Cut top from garlic bulbs and drizzle with olive oil.
Make a foil packet and wrap garlic. Bake both garlic and peppers in 400° F oven for 30-40 minutes or until pepper skin begins to blacken and blister.

Cool peppers in a container with a lid (this will help the skin loosen). Peel peppers, saving liquid. Squeeze garlic bulbs into food processor with peppers and liquid. Blend until still chunky.

Add puree, broth, tomato, tomato soup, balsamic vinegar, sugar, paprika and chipotle pepper in soup pot. Bring to a boil, reduce heat. Add green beans and cooked rice simmer until beans are tender. Taste and adjust seasonings. Garnish with minced parsley.

Serves 6

Roasted Tomato Soup

- 8 Roma tomatoes cut in half or 5 beefsteak tomatoes, quartered
- 2 whole garlic cloves
- 1 Tbsp olive oil
- 1 medium chopped onion
- 1 Tbsp grated ginger
- 4 cups vegetarian chicken broth
- 1 cup V8 juice

Heat oven to 400° F - 425° F.

Cut tomatoes in half or quarters, press peeled garlic into hollows of tomato and drizzle with olive oil. Bake for about 45 minutes until tomatoes are soft and lightly darkened.

In a soup pot, add oil, chopped onion and ginger. Sauté until onion is lightly caramelized. Add stock, V8 juice, cooked tomato and garlic. Bring to a boil.

Puree with a hand blender to desired consistency. If using a table top blender, use caution blending hot liquid. It's best to quick chill hot item to be blended.

You can make this into a pasta sauce by cutting down on the broth.

Serves 4

Roasted Vegetable Stock

Roasting vegetables before making a stock will give a much richer flavour to the soup

- 1 Tbsp olive oil
- 2 roughly chopped carrots
- 3 ribs roughly chopped celery
- 1 roughly chopped onion
- 1 roughly chopped red pepper
- 4 cloves peeled garlic
- 12 cups cold water
- 1/2 cup roughly chopped parsley
- 1 bay leaf

Preheat oven to 400° F.

Put carrots, celery, onion, red pepper and garlic on baking sheet. Toss with olive oil. Bake 30-40 minutes or until vegetables turn brown around the edges.

Remove pan from oven and pour 1/4 cup cold water over vegetables (this helps to deglaze the pan). Pour the vegetables into a soup pot. Add the cold water, parsley and bay leaf. Bring to a boil over high heat. Reduce heat and simmer for 2 hours.

Strain stock and chill.

Makes 8 - 10 cups

Russian Borsht

This is one of many borsht recipes. Enjoy.

- 2 cups water
- 1 medium potato, peeled and cubed
- 1 large carrot, peeled and diced
- 1 small beet, peeled and cubed
- 1 small onion, chopped
- 1 tsp salt

- 1 Tbsp olive oil
- 1/2 cup chopped onion
- 1 cup shredded cabbage, sautéed
- 1 Tbsp water
- 1 cup water
- 1 Tbsp dried or fresh chopped dill
- 1 tsp garlic salt
- 2 cups canned whole tomatoes, drained and chopped
- 1/2 cup shredded carrots
- 1/4 cup diced beets
- 1/4 cup diced celery
- 1/2 cup diced raw potatoes
- 3 cups canned tomatoes
- 1/2 cup raw cashews
- 1 cup water
- 1/2 cup fresh minced dill or parsley

Part 1

In a two-quart saucepan, bring water to boil. Add vegetables and simmer until tender. Drain water. Reserve some water for blending. Place cooked vegetables, water and salt in blender and blend until smooth. It's best to quick chill hot items to be blended. Set aside.

Part 2

In a 3-quart saucepan, sauté onions in olive oil until onion is translucent.
Add cabbage separately and sauté for several minutes. Add water and seasonings and bring to a boil. Add all vegetables to boiling water and simmer until tender. Add blended vegetables from Part 1 and continue simmering 5 minutes. Blend cashews with 1 cup water until smooth and creamy. Add slowly to soup and simmer for 5 minutes. Garnish with fresh minced dill or parsley and serve.

Serves 8

Sun-Dried Tomato and Garbanzo Soup

This soup is so satisfying. It always gets good reviews.

- 1 medium onion, minced
- 2 garlic cloves, minced
- 1 large carrot, minced
- 1 tsp cumin
- 1 Tbsp toasted sesame oil
- 4 cups cooked chickpeas or 2-19 oz cans
- 1-28 oz can diced tomatoes
- 5-6 chopped sun-dried tomatoes (oil packed)
- 1 tsp Dijon mustard
- 1/8 tsp cayenne pepper
- 1 tsp roasted garlic and peppers seasoning
- 1/2 Tbsp apple cider vinegar
- 1 Tbsp sodium reduced soy sauce
- 2 cups vegetarian chicken broth (see Soup Making Tips)
- 2 Tbsp almond or peanut butter
- 1/4 cup minced fresh cilantro
- 1/4 cup minced fresh parsley
- 1/4 cup minced fresh cilantro

In a soup pot, on medium heat, sauté the onions, garlic, carrots and cumin in sesame oil until carrots and onions begin to caramelize.

Puree chickpeas, tomatoes, onion, carrot mixture and some broth (for easier blending) using a blender or food processor. Do this in small batches for a smoother product. Pour puree into soup pot. Add mustard, cayenne, roasted garlic and peppers seasoning, cider vinegar, soy sauce and remaining broth. Bring to a boil. Reduce heat to medium low. Stir in nut butter and cilantro.

Simmer for 30-40 minutes or until soup becomes thick and creamy.

Taste and adjust seasonings. Stir in parsley and cilantro. Simmer for 5 minutes and serve.

Makes 6 servings

Notes:

Vegetables

Vegetables

Yam Fries, Red Pepper Aioli

Balsamic Roasted Potatoes

- 2 lbs potatoes, cubed
- 1 red bell pepper–peeled, seeded and halved
- 1 garlic bulb, roasted
- 1/3 cup extra virgin olive oil
- 3 green onions, chopped
- 1/2 cup balsamic vinegar

Preheat oven to 400° F. Line baking sheet with foil. Arrange peppers on sheet and bake until skin blackens. Blackened peppers will peel easily if put into a covered container and cooled.

Cut top from garlic bulb, drizzle with olive oil, wrap in a foil packet and place in oven with peppers. Garlic, when ready, should squeeze out easily from bulb (about 35 minutes).

Parboil cubed potatoes until al dente. Drain. Toss with a small amount of olive oil. Bake in 400° F oven until golden brown. Transfer to serving platter.

Dressing: Blend roasted garlic and olive oil together and drizzle over potatoes.

Julienne the roasted peppers and arrange on top of potatoes. Garnish with green onions. Drizzle with balsamic vinegar.

Serve at room temperature, or chilled.

Serves 6 - 8

Braised Red Cabbage

- 2 Tbsp oil
- 4 cups julienned red cabbage
- 2 cups cubed, peeled apple
- 1/4 cup organic cane sugar
- 1/4 cup vinegar
- 1/4 cup water
- 1 1/4 tsp salt
- 1/2 tsp caraway or fresh ground black pepper (optional)

Heat oil in a large pan. Stir in all the ingredients. Cover and cook over medium-low heat 15 minutes for crisp cabbage or 20-30 minutes for softer cabbage. Stir occasionally while cooking.

Serves 5

Cooked Greens

This dish is also known as Saag in Indian cooking. It is a wonderful way to eat your greens.

- 5 cups mustard greens or Chinese greens (gai lan, bok choy)
- 5 cups spinach or Swiss chard
- 1/2 cup water
- 1/4 cup whole wheat flour
- 1 Tbsp olive oil
- 1 Tbsp organic cane sugar
- 1 tsp garam masala (see Glossary)
- pinch of cayenne
- 2 Tbsp grated ginger
- 1 tsp salt

Wash greens well in several changes of water.
Remove tough stalks and chop crosswise in 1/2 inch lengths.
Heat water in a large pot.
Add chopped greens and stir constantly as greens wilt.

When the greens have shrunk considerably, move them off to the side of the pan, making a well in the centre of the pot.

Add the whole wheat flour, olive oil garam masala, cane sugar, cayenne, ginger and salt. Mix this together while incorporating the greens a little at a time. Stir to keep flour from forming lumps. Cook for about 5 minutes to cook the starch in the flour. A small addition of water may be needed depending on moisture released from the greens. Adjust seasonings.

Serves 6

Curried Cabbage

This dish can be turned into a soup by adding chicken style soup broth to the pot and simmering until heated.

- 3 Tbsp vegetable oil
- 1 medium onion, thinly sliced
- 1 tsp ground cumin
- 1 tsp ginger grated
- 2 tsp curry paste
- 1 tsp ground mustard seeds
- 4 cups coarsely shredded cabbage
- 1 cup coarsely grated carrots
- 1/2 cup finely sliced red bell pepper
- 1/2 tsp salt or to taste
- 1 cup green peas
- 1/4 cup chopped cilantro

In a large saucepan, heat oil.
Add onions, cumin, ginger, curry paste, and mustard seeds. Fry until onion is translucent.
Add cabbage, red pepper, carrots and salt.

Cook over medium heat, stirring for 5 minutes. Cover pan, set heat to medium/low and cook until vegetables are tender but not soft. In last few minutes of cooking, add peas.

Serve garnished with cilantro.

Serves 6

Curry Glazed Tomatoes

Roasting tomatoes brings out their flavour. Glazing with this sauce makes them even more delicious!

- 2 Tbsp olive oil
- 1/2 cup minced onion
- 1 cup tomato juice
- 1/4 cup orange marmalade
- 1 tsp curry powder or curry paste
- 1/2 tsp ground cinnamon
- 1/2 tsp sea salt or to taste
- 1/4 tsp fresh ground pepper or pinch of cayenne pepper
- 6 large tomatoes
- 3 cups hot cooked rice (optional)

Heat olive oil over medium heat. Add onion and sauté lightly.
Add curry and cinnamon, stirring to release flavours.
Add tomato juice, marmalade, salt and pepper. Bring sauce to a boil.
Remove from heat and set aside.

Remove the hard core and seeds from tomatoes.
Arrange the whole tomatoes in a buttered 2-quart size baking dish.
Pour sauce over the tomatoes. (If you make this dish ahead of time, cover and refrigerate.)

Bake uncovered in a 400° F oven until tomatoes are just tender when pierced with a fork (about 20-25 minutes, if refrigerated).

To serve, arrange tomatoes on a bed of rice or quinoa and spoon remaining sauce over all.

Serves 6

Curried Cabbage

Glazed Beans

- 2 lbs green beans
- 1/4 tsp dried vegetable seasoning (see Glossary)
- 1/2 Tbsp olive oil

Take ends off beans. Blanch for one minute (see Cooking Terms).
Heat oil in frying pan and sauté with seasoning. Add blanched beans. Cook until al dente. (see Cooking Terms)

Serves 6 - 8

Glazed Carrots

- 10 medium carrots peeled
- 1 Tbsp maple syrup
- 1/2 tsp Greek seasoning (see Glossary)
- 1 Tbsp oil or non-dairy butter

Cut carrots in half, lengthwise. Blanch for one minute (see Cooking Terms).
Place in baking dish. Add syrup and seasoning. Dot with non-dairy butter.
Bake at 350° F, covered for 1 hour.

Serves 6 - 8

Golden Scalloped Potatoes

- 4 medium potatoes
- 1 small onion, sliced
- 2 cups water
- 2/3 cup raw cashews
- 2 Tbsp unbleached white flour
- pinch of cayenne
- 1 tsp salt (or to taste)
- 1/3 cup soy parmesan cheese
- paprika
- 2 Tbsp non-dairy butter

Peel and slice potatoes into thin scallops. Lightly sauté onion slices in a little olive oil.

Layer potato scallops and onion rings in the bottom of a casserole dish sprayed with vegetable oil. Place water, cashews, flour, cayenne, salt andparmesan cheese in blender and blend until smooth. Pour mixture in pot and cook over medium heat, stirring constantly, until mixture comes to a boil. Pour sauce over potatoes.

Sprinkle with paprika.
Dot butter over top of potatoes.
Bake in a preheated oven at 375° F for 1 to 1 1/2 hours.

Note: If sauce does not cover the potatoes completely, pour tofu milk over the mixture before putting it into the oven. Turn oven down to 350° F when the potatoes start to bubble.

Serves 4 - 6

Greek Potatoes

- 20 Yukon Gold nugget potatoes
- 2 Tbsp olive oil
- 1 Tbsp lemon juice
- 1 Tbsp lemon herb seasoning (see Glossary)

Clean and parboil potatoes on medium heat for 10 minutes. Drain and slice in half or quarter.
Toss potatoes with oil, lemon, and lemon herb seasoning.

Bake at 350° F for about 35 minutes on a baking sheet in one layer, so they will fry and not steam.

Serves 6 - 8

Oven Fried Potatoes Soaking Method

- 6 large russet, red or Yukon Gold potatoes
- grapeseed oil
- paprika (Hungarian or smoked)
- salt
- cayenne pepper
- black pepper

Peel potatoes and cut into wedges. Fill a large pot with water and soak cut potatoes with 1 tsp salt overnight. Drain water and towel dry the potatoes. Preheat oven to 450° F.
Add olive oil and seasonings (according to your taste) to a bowl with the potatoes and coat all potatoes evenly. Spread out on baking sheets, leaving spaces between potatoes so they fry – not steam.

Bake for 15 minutes on lowest oven rack. Turn over and bake for 15-20 minutes longer until golden brown.

Serves 4

Oven Fried Potatoes
Parboiling Method

- 6 large russet, red or Yukon Gold potatoes
- grapeseed oil
- paprika (Hungarian or smoked)
- salt
- cayenne pepper
- black pepper

Peel potatoes and cut into wedges.
Fill a large pot with salted water and bring to a boil.
Add potato wedges and parboil until the outer layer of potato begins to cook (about 4 minutes). Drain and towel dry.
Heat oven to 450° F. Add olive oil and seasonings (according to your taste) to a large bowl with the potatoes and coat all potatoes evenly. Spread out on a baking sheet, leaving spaces between potatoes so they will fry-not steam.
Bake for 15 minutes on lowest rack.
Turn potatoes over and bake for 15-20 minutes longer until golden brown.
Serves 4

Savoury Green Beans

- 2 Tbsp olive oil
- 5 cups beans cut French style
- 2 cloves garlic finely chopped
- 2 tsp organic cane sugar
- 1/4 tsp Hungarian paprika (hot)
- 1/2 cup chopped cilantro
- 2-3 Tbsp water

Heat oil over medium heat in large sauté pan.
Stir in green beans, garlic, organic cane sugar, paprika and cilantro.
Stir-fry 45 seconds.
Pour in water and cover to steam until green beans are tender.
Variation: use trimmed sliced brussels sprouts.

Serves 6 - 8

Soy Glazed Turnips
Turnips never tasted so good.

- 2 Tbsp olive oil
- 4 cups turnips
- 5 Tbsp water
- 2 tsp sodium reduced soy sauce

Select turnips that are small to medium sized with firm, smooth skin.
Peel and cut into thin, bite sized pieces.

Heat olive oil in a heavy, wide sauté pan.
Add turnips and sauté for 3-4 minutes until turnips are slightly glazed.
Add water and soy sauce.
Cover and cook over medium-low heat for 5-10 minutes or until turnips are tender. Stir occasionally while cooking.

Serves 6

Stir Fried Vegetables

- 1 Tbsp grapeseed oil
- 1-2 Tbsp fresh grated ginger
- 1-2 cloves garlic, grated
- 1/4 cup water or chicken-style broth

Sauce

- 2 tsp sesame oil
- 2 Tbsp water
- 1 Tbsp sodium reduced soy sauce
- 1 Tbsp black bean sauce
- 1 Tbsp rice starch or cornstarch

To prepare vegetables for stir frying, cut them on a diagonal, Chinese style. A wok is handy, but you can also use a large skillet. Cook the vegetables in batches if your pan will not hold all the vegetables at once. Start with those vegetables that take the longest to cook and end with the more delicate ones.

Prepare 6 cups of any combination: bok choy, broccoli, carrot, celery, Chinese cabbage, gailan, mushrooms, onions, snap peas, peppers, zucchini, bamboo shoots, water chestnuts, bean sprouts.

Heat grapeseed oil in a wok on high heat. Begin stir frying vegetables that take longest to cook. Gradually add remaining vegetables so they are all cooked – tender yet crisp. Add ginger and garlic. If pan dries out and needs more oil, use water or chicken broth to replace oil.

Mix the sauce ingredients together and add to vegetables. Stir fry for about 3-5 minutes. The sauce will turn glossy when the starch has been cooked.

Serve with grains or noodles.

Serves 6 - 8

Tilly's Potatoes

- 8 cooked (but still firm) medium whole potatoes peeled
- 1 small onion
- 2/3 cup raw cashews
- 1/4 tsp celery salt
- 1/2 tsp onion powder
- 1/4 tsp salt
- 3/4 cup water
- paprika
- fresh dill for garnish

Preheat oven to 350° F.

Grate potatoes with coarse grater and place in bowl. Grate onion with fine grater and mix together with potatoes.

Place cashews, celery salt and onion powder in blender. Add water and blend until very smooth and creamy.

Pour blended mixture over potatoes and onions and mix together.

Place potatoes in an oiled 9 x 13 inch casserole dish. Sprinkle with paprika. Cover and bake for 45 minutes.

Garnish with chopped fresh dill.

Serves 6

Twice Baked Potatoes

- 6 baking potatoes
- 1/4 cup non-dairy butter
- 1/4 cup soy cream cheese
- 1/4 cup soy cheddar cheese
- 1 Tbsp parmesan cheese
- 1 Tbsp tofu milk (or milk of choice)
- sea salt or preferred seasoning

Preheat oven to 375° F

Scrub potatoes and place on a cookie sheet. Bake one hour or until tender when pierced with a fork.

Drop oven temperature to 350° F

When potatoes are cool enough to handle, cut around the top of the potato.
Remove this piece of potato and scoop the flesh from the skin.
Mash the potato, non-dairy butter, cream cheese, cheddar cheese, parmesan cheese, milk and seasoning.

Refill the potato skins with the creamed potato mixture.

Return to oven and bake for 30 minutes at 350° F.

If preparing ahead of time, refrigerate.

Serves 6

Vegetable Root Bake

- 2 cups sweet potatoes or yams
- 1/2 fennel bulb (optional)
- 4 carrots
- 2 parsnips
- 2 beets
- 1 red onion
- 2 red bell peppers
- 2 Tbsp balsamic vinegar
- 2 Tbsp olive oil
- 1 Tbsp fresh rosemary
- 1/2 Tbsp organic cane sugar
- sea salt, cayenne or black pepper to season

Peel sweet potatoes, carrots, onion, parsnips, and beets.
Trim fennel. Core and seed peppers. Cut veggies into bite sized pieces.

Beets take longer to bake; use a separate pan for them. Drizzle with olive oil. Bake until fork tender-about 60 minutes.

Place other veggies in a bowl and drizzle with olive oil, balsamic vinegar, rosemary and sugar.

Layer on a baking sheet, leaving space between vegetables, so they roast and not steam. (Use two baking sheets, if needed). Rotate half way through cooking time.

Bake at 425° F for 35-40 minutes.
Serve hot or at room temperature.
Brussels sprouts, eggplant, squash, zucchini and turnip are also nice roasted.

Serves 6

Vegetable Root Bake

Yam Fries

These are delicious served with Red Pepper Aioli or Roasted Red Pepper Dip

- 6 cups yams
- 1/2 tsp fresh ground black pepper or cayenne pepper
- 1 tsp dried vegetable seasoning (try spicy mesquite or roasted red peppers and garlic)
- 2 Tbsp olive oil

Preheat oven to 425°. Cut yams into French fry size or smaller.
Sprinkle seasonings and oil in large bowl.
Add yams and toss ingredients together.
Spread yams on baking sheet, leaving spaces between them so they will fry, not steam.

Bake on lowest oven rack for 20-25 minutes. Turn halfway during baking time and bake until golden. These fries won't crisp as with white potato fries.

Serves 4 - 6

Notes:

Light Meals

Light Meals

Bruschetta

Asian Noodle Salad

A wonderful salad that looks so appealing.

Marinade
- 1/4 cup olive oil
- 1/2 cup orange juice
- 1/4 cup sodium reduced soy sauce
- 1 tsp dry mustard
- 1 Tbsp toasted sesame oil
- 1 tsp ground ginger or 1 Tbsp fresh ginger
- 1 Tbsp curry paste
- 1/4 cup fresh cilantro

Salad
- 375 g package of whole wheat spaghetti
- 12 fresh, Chinese-cut snow peas, blanched
- 1 cup peeled and julienned carrots, blanched
- 1 julienned red bell pepper
- 2 julienned green onions
- 1 cup julienned jicama (or peeled, julienned broccoli stalks)
- 1 cup sliced mushrooms
- 1 head romaine lettuce
- 1 cup alfalfa sprouts
- 1/4 cup toasted sesame seeds

Marinade: Add all ingredients to a blender, process until smooth.

Salad: Cook the noodles until al dente then toss with marinade in a large bowl. Refrigerate until chilled.

Blanch snow peas and carrots, drop in cold water bath, drain and add to the noodles.

Prepare red pepper, green onion, jicama and mushrooms.
Add these vegetables to the noodle mixture. Toss lightly.

Arrange shredded lettuce on a serving platter.

Top lettuce with marinated noodle mixture and garnish with sprouts and sesame seeds.

Serves 6 - 8

Asian Noodle Salad

Bruschetta

- 1 multigrain baguette (or your choice of artisan bread)
- 1 1/2 cups seeded and coarsely chopped tomatoes
- 1/2 cup chopped green onions
- 1/4 cup freshly chopped parsley or basil or a combination of both
- 1/4 cup chopped black or Kalamata pitted olives
- 3 Tbsp extra virgin olive oil
- 1/2 tsp salt
- 2 cloves of garlic, grated
- freshly ground pepper, to taste
- 1/2 cup soy parmesan cheese
- 1/2 cup soy mozzarella cheese
- 1/4 cup chopped fresh parsley

Slice the bread and toast lightly.

Mix the tomatoes, onions, parsley, olives, basil, oil, salt, garlic, and pepper. Add parmesan and mozzarella cheese.

Place spoonfuls onto the bread. Arrange on a parchment-lined cookie sheet. We suggest you line baking sheets when broiling soy cheeses for easier cleanup.

Broil for several minutes, allowing the cheese to melt.

Serve garnished with fresh parsley.

Serves 6 - 8

Curried Garbanzos

This is a favourite. Rich and creamy with a nice balance of spices.

- 1 medium onion, minced
- 2 cloves garlic, minced
- 1 Tbsp curry paste
- 1 Tbsp garam masala (see Glossary)
- 2 tsp cumin
- 2 Tbsp flour
- 1-398 ml (14 oz) can coconut milk
- 2 Tbsp chicken style soup base
- 1-540 ml (19 oz) can garbanzos (chick peas), drained and rinsed.
- 2 medium tomatoes, seeded and diced or 2 cups diced canned tomato, drained
- 1/4 cup chopped cilantro
- 1 Tbsp fresh lemon juice

Sauté onions and garlic in oil until soft.

Add spices and sauté.

Stir in the flour. Cook for several minutes, stirring constantly.

Add coconut milk and chicken soup base, stirring to make a sauce.

Add diced tomatoes and garbanzos, breaking up some garbanzos with your hands. Cook over medium low heat for 30-40 minutes. Add cilantro and lemon. Taste and adjust seasonings. Simmer for 10 minutes.

If you prefer a thicker consistency, add another can of chickpeas.

Garnish with minced fresh cilantro.

Serve over rice, with samosas or flatbread.

Serves 4 - 6

Empanadas
A spicy Spanish turnover.

- 1 recipe of Basic Pie Crust (see Desserts)
- 1/2 cup minced onion
- 2 cloves minced garlic
- 1 tsp ground cumin
- 1 tsp canned chipotle pepper, minced
- 1 tsp chilli powder
- 2 1/2 cups (19 oz can) black beans
- 1 1/2 cups crushed, strained tomatoes
- 1 pkg (340 g) veggie ground (see Glossary)
- 1 Tbsp minced fresh cilantro

In a heavy frying pan, sauté onions and garlic over medium heat for several minutes. Add cumin, chipotle and chilli. Sauté until the spices become scented. Mash the black beans in the pan with a fork or potato masher. Add the crushed tomatoes and veggie ground crumble into small pieces. Simmer on medium low heat for about 20 minutes. Stir in chopped cilantro. Cool mixture before making empanadas.

Preheat oven to 400° F

To make empanadas:
Roll pastry on a lightly floured board to 1/8 inch thickness and cut out 4 inch rounds. Place 2 Tbsp of cooled filling in the center of each round and fold pastry over. Dip fork in cold water and press dough edges together. Poke the top of each empanada with the fork. Place on a baking sheet 1 inch apart. Bake for 15-20 minutes. Serve warm with salsa.

Note: This filling can also be used for quesadillas or tacos.

Makes 24

Fajitas

This is fast, easy, and a delicious wrap.

- 1-227 g package meatless chicken or beef strips (see Glossary)
- 1 large onion, sliced thin
- 2 ribs celery, sliced thin
- 2 coloured bell peppers, sliced thin
- 1 clove garlic, minced
- 2 tsp chilli powder
- 1 tsp chipotle powder or canned chipotle pepper
- 1/2 tsp ground cumin
- 1 cup prepared tomato salsa
- 1 cup soy cheddar
- 6-10 inch whole grain tortilla shells

Cut chicken strips into bite-size pieces. Fry in small amount of oil until golden. Remove strips from pan. Add small amount of oil to pan and sauté onion, celery and bell peppers for several minutes.
Add grated garlic, chilli powder, chipotle and cumin. Sauté until vegetables are cooked.
Stir in prepared salsa and chicken strips.
Meanwhile, heat tortilla shells in a warm oven or on a dry frying pan over medium heat.
Scoop a spoonful of fajita mixture in the center of tortilla shell, sprinkle with soy cheddar, and roll.

Serve with soy sour cream, guacamole or salsa.

Note: Use 7 inch tortilla shells for smaller portions.

Serves 6

Falafels

Our version of these Middle-Eastern patties are easy to make and full of flavour.

- 1 - 19 oz can chickpeas, drained
- 1/2 cup finely minced onion
- 2 cloves grated garlic
- 2 tsp ground cumin
- 1 tsp ground coriander
- 1/2 tsp salt
- pinch cayenne pepper
- 1 Tbsp olive oil
- 1/2 cup chopped fresh parsley
- 1 Tbsp lemon juice
- 1 cup fresh bread crumbs
- 1/2 cup medium tofu, mashed

Rinse the chickpeas and drain well.

In a large bowl, mash the chickpeas until thick and pasty.

Sauté the onion, garlic, cumin, coriander, salt and cayenne until the onion is golden brown. Stir into the chickpeas along with the olive oil: parsley, lemon juice, tofu and bread crumbs. Adjust oil or breadcrumbs until the mixture holds together.

Scoop 2 Tbsp of mixture and flatten into a patty. Patty paper or wax paper works well for assembly.

You can cook falafel as you make them or store the mixture in a tightly covered container in the refrigerator for several days.

Heat a heavy skillet on medium heat. Add oil to cover the bottom. Drop patties into hot oil and cook for about 4 minutes on each side. Keep patties warm in a 300° F oven until serving time.

Serve in warm pita breads with condiments such as tzaziki, grated carrot, sliced tomato, cucumber or chopped lettuce .

Serves 6

Fresh Veggie Pizza

- 1 cup soy cream cheese
- 1/2 cup vegan mayonnaise
- 1/2 cup soy sour cream
- 4 cloves crushed garlic
- 2 tsp dried vegetable seasoning
- 1 cup chopped green onion
- 1 cup grated carrot
- 1 cup diced red pepper
- 1 cup sliced, pitted black olives
- 1/2 cup blanched broccoli florettes, broken into small pieces
- 1/2 cup chopped parsley

Make Quick Pizza Dough (see recipe page 186)

Spread on sprayed baking sheets (makes two sheets)

Bake at 450° for 8-10 minutes or until done. Flip the dough over halfway through baking, if dough cooks unevenly.

Mix together soy cream cheese, vegan mayonnaise, soy sour cream, crushed garlic, and dried vegetable seasoning.

Spread this creamed mixture over cooled pizza crust.

Sprinkle over green onion, grated carrot, red pepper, black olives, broccoli florettes and parsley over creamed mixture:

Trim crusts, cut into rectangular pieces.

Serves 12

Garlic Black Bean and Tofu

This is a meal in itself, or serve it with stir fried vegetables.

- 2 cups (227 g) commercial soy beef or chicken strips
- 1 small onion, halved and sliced
- 1 Tbsp sodium reduced soy sauce or black bean sauce

Sauce

- 2 Tbsp olive oil
- 1 onion, halved and sliced
- 1 Tbsp organic cane sugar
- 1 Tbsp vinegar
- 1 cup fresh orange juice
- 1/4 cup plum sauce
- 1 tsp black bean garlic sauce

- 1-400 g package eggless Chinese noodles
- 4 cups Chinese greens- bok choy, gai lan, snow peas
- 1/2 cup julienned red pepper

Cut strips into thinner strips. Sauté the onion in a small amount of olive oil until transparent. Add strips and season with a 1 Tbsp of soy sauce or black bean garlic sauce. Set aside.

Heat a wok to medium high. Add olive oil, onion and sugar. Cook until golden (about 10 minutes). Add vinegar, orange juice, plum and black bean sauce. Bring to a boil. Reduce heat. Add beef strips. Simmer.

Sauté greens until tender, but still bright green. Add to the sauce, saving some for garnishing. Sauté red pepper for garnishing. Cook noodles according to package directions. Arrange the noodles on a serving platter. Drizzle sauce over top and toss to keep the noodles from sticking together. Pour remaining sauce over noodles. Garnish with the reserved greens and sautéed red pepper.

Serves 6 - 8

- 6 whole grain artisan bread rolls or panini flat bread
- soy cheeses, (feta, cheddar, mozzarella) as much as desired
- mustards or Red Bell Pepper Puree (see recipe page 114) for spreading on bread
- 350 g package of marinated tofu, sliced into thin pieces
- grilled vegetables of your choice such as peppers, zucchini, onions, artichokes, sun-dried tomato, green onion, jalapenos, any of your favourite vegetables.

Marinating Sauce for Tofu Recipe

- 1/3 cup red wine vinegar
- 2 Tbsp olive oil
- 1 Tbsp balsamic vinegar

Grilled Panini

Mix ingredients for marinating sauce and pour over the tofu and vegetables, letting it marinate for about 2 hours. Drain marinade and quickly brown vegetables and tofu in a hot skillet.

Lay out bread, spread with mustard or red bell pepper puree. Arrange cooked marinated mixture and cheese on bread slices.

Lightly brush panini with olive oil.

Fry the sandwich in a skillet, using a spatula to press down on the sandwich while toasting (or use a panini grill).

Serves 6

Lettuce Wraps

A tasty bundle for a hot summer day.

- 2 heads iceberg lettuce
- 1 pkg vegetarian chicken strips, julienned (1 cup) or
- 1 pkg marinated firm tofu, julienned (see Cooking Terms)
- 1 Tbsp grapeseed oil
- 1 Tbsp sesame oil
- 1 cup julienned (1 1/2 inch-4 cm) coloured bell peppers
- 1 cup carrots, julienned (as above)
- 1/2 cup chopped green or red onion
- 1 cup chopped celery
- 1 Tbsp fresh grated ginger
- 2 Tbsp sodium reduced soy sauce
- 1 Tbsp Dijon mustard
- 1/4 cup Thai sweet chilli sauce
- 1/2 tsp Chinese Five Spice powder (optional)
- 1/2 cup chopped cilantro
- 4 cups eggless Chinese noodles (steam-fried type)
- 1/2 cup almonds sliced (optional)

Core lettuce and carefully remove leaves (running water helps loosen the leaves). For this recipe, use the inner cupped leaves. Save outer leaves for a tossed salad. Invert the lettuce cups on dish towels to drain. On a baking sheet, roast noodles under a low heat broiler, tossing several times until golden brown. Do the same thing with the almonds if using them. Keep an eye on broiling items to prevent burning. Heat a wok or large pan over medium high heat. Add grapeseed and sesame oil. Add vegetarian strips (or tofu) and onions. Fry until golden. Add peppers, carrots, celery and ginger. Sauté until al dente. Mix together soy sauce, Dijon mustard, Thai chilli sauce, Chinese Five Spice and cilantro. Add to the stir fry and toss together. Add the noodles to the stir fry mixture. Spoon into lettuce cups. Wrap burrito style and enjoy.

Note: If you want to serve with a dipping sauce, see Peanut Butter dipping sauce recipe.

Serves 8 - 10

Pesto Bundles
These little bundles are loaded with herbal delight.

- 1 cup soy mozzarella, grated
- 3 Tbsp pesto sauce (see recipe page 108)
- 4 phyllo pastry sheets
- 2 Tbsp olive oil

Mix cheese and pesto sauce together. Remove four phyllo sheets from package and rewrap unused sheets well.

Cut the phyllo sheets into 3 inch squares. Lay one square at an angle over another square, forming an 8 pointed star. Brush olive oil on the points.

Place a teaspoon of the cheese, pesto mixture in the center of each square. Gather the corners together and twist lightly to make a bundle. Place on a cookie sheet and bake at 375° for 5-8 minutes.

Makes 20 bundles

Phyllo Samosas

Using phyllo pastry makes these samosas lighter than the traditional pastry.

- 4 Tbsp olive oil
- 2 cloves minced garlic
- 1 cup finely chopped onion
- 1 tsp grated fresh ginger
- 1 Tbsp curry paste or powder
- 1 Tbsp garam masala
- 2 cups peeled 1/4 inch cut potatoes cooked al dente
- 2 tsp fresh lemon juice
- 1 cup green peas fresh or frozen
- 1 Tbsp chopped fresh cilantro
- salt to taste

Heat large frying pan. Sauté garlic and onion and fry until translucent. Add ginger, curry, and garam masala . Mix together to combine the flavours. Do not brown. Sauté until spices become aromatic. Add to cooked potatoes.

Add lemon juice and cilantro. Add salt to taste and adjust seasonings.

Add the peas and set aside to cool.

Defrost one 454 g package of phyllo pastry. (Doubling the filling uses one whole package of phyllo pastry.)

Remove one phyllo sheet from the pile. Brush with olive oil and fold in thirds length-wise.

Drop 2 Tbsp of filling on outer corner of folded pastry and fold as you would a flag, or corner to corner.

Brush the top with olive oil and bake at 375° F for 25-30 minutes, or until golden. Serve with Mint Chutney (see recipe page 105).

Note: When using phyllo pastry open up the folded sheets of phyllo, cover completely with parchment or wax paper then put a lightly damp towel on top. This keeps the phyllo from drying out and becoming brittle.

Serves 6 - 8

Polenta Pizza

A great variation to a wheat crust

- 4 cups vegetarian chicken stock
- 1 cup coarse polenta (cornmeal)
- 1 tsp roasted garlic red peppers seasoning (optional)
- 2 Tbsp non-dairy butter substitute, softened
- 1/2 cup grated soy parmesan

Bring 4 cups of stock to the boil. Reduce heat and slowly whisk in 1 cup of polenta. Continue whisking for five minutes. Replace whisk with a wooden spoon and stir until spoon can stand and polenta pulls away from the sides of the pan. Stir in 2 Tbsp of butter substitute and soy parmesan.
Remove from heat and let cool until mixture can be handled comfortably.

Preheat oven to 400° F

Spread the polenta mixture over an oiled baking sheet or pizza pan. Bake for ten minutes in 400° F oven. Remove from oven and spread with pesto sauce, red pepper sauce or pizza sauce, leaving 1/2 inch border around the dough.
Build pizza with your favourite toppings and sprinkle with grated soy mozzarella.

Bake for 15-20 minutes, or until cheese is melted.

Serves 6

Quick Thin Crust Pizza

With this thin crust recipe, you can be eating pizza within 30 minutes.

Dough

- 3/4 cup unbleached flour
- 1/2 cup whole wheat flour
- 1 Tbsp olive oil
- 1/2 tsp salt
- 2 tsp dry yeast
- 1/2 cup warm water

Preheat oven to 450° F

Dissolve yeast in water, let stand for 5 minutes. Add olive oil and salt. Gradually beat in flour. Knead dough until it pulls away from the bowl. Knead on lightly floured surface for about 3 minutes. The dough is ready to make into pizza

A baking stone or pizza stone is a valuable tool to have in your kitchen. You can also use it to make artisan style breads. Follow the directions that come with the stone. Preheat the oven for 45 minutes with the stone placed on the lowest rack in the oven. The stone must be hot to cook the pizza quickly. You will need a pizza paddle to transfer the dough to the stone. We use a sideless non-stick baking sheet or the bottom of a baking sheet. Make sure that the pizza can slide off easily. Use a generous amount of cornmeal to dust the pan. Roll out the dough on a floured surface. Transfer it to the cornmeal dredged paddle. Slide dough onto the hot stone. Bake for 6 to 8 minutes. Remove dough from oven. Add toppings and cheese and return to oven. If not using a baking stone, press dough into a cornmeal dusted pan, bake for 6-8 minutes, remove from oven and add sauce and toppings. Return to oven. Bake for 10 minutes at 450° F.

Makes one 12-inch pizza crust

Sauces for Quick Thin Crust Pizza

Use traditional tomato sauce, pesto sauce or try the red pepper aioli or roasted red pepper sauce.

Toppings: Can include cooked asparagus, canned artichokes, sun dried tomatoes, fresh tomatoes, olives, jalapenos, green onions, caramelized onions, sweet peppers, fresh basil, parsley, arugula, spinach, veggie pepperoni, salami, fried meatless chicken strips.

Soy cheeses: mozzarella, cheddar, feta, parmesan

Make pizza the Italian method and limit your toppings to three or four items.

Note: If you prefer a thicker crust pizza, look for a recipe with a longer proofing time then follow the same procedure for baking (see Italian Breadstick recipe page 53).

Rice Paper Wraps
Refreshing on a hot summer day.

Tips on preparing rice paper wraps:

Place a moistened kitchen towel on the counter to keep rice paper from sticking to counter.
Warm water will be needed to soften the rice paper.

To keep the water at a constant temperature, use a pan of water on stovetop with the temperature set on low. The constant warm temperature speeds up the softening of rice paper.

Do not let rice paper sit too long in water or it becomes too soft.

When the rice paper is pliable, it is ready to use.

Roll up whatever filling you choose into a burrito or cabbage roll style bundle. Rolls can be made up to three hours ahead of serving time.

Serve rice paper wraps with dipping sauces (see recipe page 123).
Use 6 inch wraps for smaller servings or 8 inch wraps for larger servings.
Count on 3 smaller wraps or 2 larger wraps per serving.

Filling for Rice Paper Wraps

- julienned carrots, cucumbers, daikon radish
- julienned lettuce, Chinese cabbage (sui choy)
- julienned green onion
- minced cilantro
- sprouts
- marinated firm tofu, fried

Combine all the ingredients used for a filling. Use tongs to transfer filling to the rice paper. For wrapping use about 2-3 Tbsp of filling per wrap. Serve on a platter or individual side plates. Garnish with minced cilantro, parsley, or sesame seeds, with a condiment cup of dipping sauce (see recipe page 123).

Spanakopita

Serve these delicious little packages with Tzatziki.

- 6 cups of fresh spinach steamed, or 1- 300g package frozen spinach, thawed and drained
- 1 cup crumbled or finely grated soy feta cheese
- 3-4 roasted garlic cloves
- salt and cayenne pepper to taste
- 2 Tbsp soy mayonnaise
- 3 sheets phyllo pastry

Using your hands, squeeze as much moisture out of the spinach as possible.
Crumble feta cheese onto the spinach.
Mash roasted garlic and seasoning with soy mayonnaise and add to spinach mixture.

Take out one sheet of phyllo pastry and brush with olive oil.
Fold width to width and cut into four strips. This will make appetizer sized portions.

Put a spoonful of mixture at end of strip. Fold like a flag (corner to corner). Brush the top with olive oil.

Place on baking sheet and repeat the above until filling is used up.
Bake at 375° F for approximately 15 minutes or until golden brown.

Spanakopitas can be frozen prior to baking. Bake directly from freezer on a baking sheet at 375° F for 20-25 minutes.

Note: While working with phyllo pastry, always keep it covered with parchment paper or wax paper and a slightly damp towel. It will dry out quickly if exposed to air.

Serves 12

Rice Paper Wraps

Spinach Wraps

- 6-10 inch tortilla wraps-
  pesto, spinach, sun-dried
  tomato or whole wheat
- 1 cup soy cream cheese
- 2 Tbsp hamburger tomato
  relish
- 2 Tbsp sweet green
  pickle relish
- 1/2 cup grated soy
  cheddar
- 1 cup chopped spinach
  leaves
- 1/2 cup chopped
  vegetarian turkey
- 1 cup finely chopped red
  and yellow peppers
- 1/2 cup minced parsley
- parsley for garnish

Blend cream cheese and relish together. Take
a stack of tortilla wraps from their package.
Cut 1/2 inch off opposite ends of tortilla
wraps. Lay shells out on counter and spread
each with cream cheese mixture.

Sprinkle spinach, cheddar, turkey, chopped
peppers and parsley over cream cheese
mixture.

Roll tortilla tightly and cut in half on a
diagonal.

Garnish with minced parsley.

Serves 6 - 12

Notes:

Entrees

Entrees

Hungarian Potato Goulash

Cabbage Rolls

- 1 large loose cabbage
- 6 cups water
- 1/2 tsp salt
- 1 recipe cabbage roll filling (see recipe)
- 2 cups tomato sauce (see recipe)

Cabbage Roll Filling

- 1 large onion
- 1 cup finely diced celery
- 1 cup raw cashews
- 1 1/2 cups water
- 2 Tbsp chicken style soup base
- 1 tsp salt
- 4 cups cooked basmati rice
- 1 cup veggie ground (see Glossary)

Sauce for Cabbage Rolls

- 3 cups tomato juice
- 1/2 can tomato soup
- 1 Tbsp maple syrup
- salt to taste

In a large pot, add salt and water and bring to a boil. Cut the core from a head of cabbage deep enough to start a separation of the outer leaves from the core. Dip the cabbage in boiling water, loosening 2 to 3 leaves. Continue dipping cabbage and removing leaves. Blanch the leaves for 2 minutes, or until pliable. Cut off some of the central leaf ribs for easier rolling. Have all leaves loosened and ready for filling.

Sauté onion and celery in a lightly oiled skillet until tender. Place cashews, water, chicken style soup base and salt in blender and blend until smooth. Add this mixture to sautéed onions and celery. Heat and stir until bubbling. In a large bowl, combine rice and veggie ground. Add blended cashew mixture and mix well.

To fill cabbage rolls: Put a spoonful of filling on the stem end of each cabbage leaf folding end and sides over the filling. Roll into a tight bundle.

Lay large broken cabbage leaves on the bottom of a casserole dish to prevent scorching. Carefully place cabbage rolls on the leaves, open end down, packing them snugly so they don't unroll.

Pour tomato sauce over the cabbage rolls. Cover the casserole dish.

Bake for 90 minutes at 325° F.

Serves 6 - 8

Cashew Rice Loaf

- 1 medium cooking onion, finely diced
- 1 cup finely ground raw cashews
- 1 cup fresh whole wheat bread crumbs
- 1 cup cooked brown rice
- 3/4 cup tofu milk (or milk of choice)
- 2 Tbsp sodium reduced soy sauce
- 1 Tbsp dried or minced fresh parsley
- 1/4 tsp celery salt
- 1/2 tsp salt or to taste

Sauté onion until translucent. Mix cashews, breadcrumbs, rice and onion together in large bowl. Add milk, soy sauce, parsley, celery salt and salt. Mixture should hold together slightly when squeezed in the palm of your hand. Lightly pack mixture in an oiled 8 x 5 x 3 inch loaf pan and bake at 350° F for approximately 40 minutes or until loaf is golden brown and firm. Rest loaf for 5 minutes before removing from pan. Turn loaf out onto serving dish and garnish with cranberry sauce and fresh parsley.

Tip: Use parchment paper strips to line pans for easy removal of loaf. Triple recipe and use a bundt pan for nice presentation.

Serves 5

Chicken Roll Ups

- 2 cups seasoned mashed potatoes
- 1 package multigrain crescent rolls, or Quick Crust Pizza Dough (see recipe page 186)
- 1 medium onion, chopped
- 1 cup chopped celery
- 1/2 cup chopped red pepper
- 1 package vegetarian chicken crumble (see Glossary)
- 1-2 Tbsp sodium reduced soy sauce
- 1-2 tsp chicken style soup base
- 1 Tbsp melted non-dairy butter

Cook the potatoes, mash them until they are creamy. Season well with salt, pepper and dry vegetable seasoning. Cool.

Sauté onion in oil until translucent. Add celery, red pepper, and broken up chicken crumble. Season with a bit of soy sauce and chicken soup base until desired flavour is reached.

Make quick pizza dough or open crescent rolls. Put rolls together to make a 9 x 13 inch rectangle and press edges firmly together so they won't separate when baking. Do this on a piece of parchment paper to make transferring to pan easier. Spread potato filling onto the dough and then spread the chicken filling.
Leave a border of exposed dough along both sides of filling. Fold the two lengths of dough together. Pinch the seam together, forming a log shape. Transfer seam side down onto the baking sheet. If using pizza dough, follow the same procedure as above. Score the roll up to mark individual servings. Brush roll with melted non-dairy butter.
Bake at 375° F for about 20-25 minutes.

Place on a platter. Slice into portion sizes. Garnish with minced parsley and serve with cranberry sauce.

Serves 6

Chicken Roll Ups

Creamy Fettuccine Alfredo

- 1-454 g box fettuccine noodles
- 1/2 cup raw cashews
- 2 cups water
- 1 Tbsp unbleached white flour
- 1 Tbsp chicken style soup base (see Glossary)
- 1/4 tsp onion powder
- 1/2 tsp salt
- 1 tsp dried basil or 1/4 cup chopped fresh basil
- 1/4 cup soy parmesan
- dash cayenne pepper

Pour cashews, water, flour, chicken soup base, onion powder and salt into blender. Add water and blend until smooth and creamy. Pour blended mixture into saucepan and bring to a slow boil. Stir to prevent scorching. Add basil, parmesan and cayenne. Remove from heat. If sauce is too thick, add a little soy milk or broth to make desired consistency.

Serve over cooked fettuccine noodles and garnish with fresh basil.

Makes 3 cups

Egg Rolls

- 1-454 g package tofu, rinsed and drained
- 3 Tbsp chicken style soup base
- 1/2 cup finely diced onion
- 1/3 cup finely diced carrot
- 1/2 cup finely diced celery
- 1 cup finely shredded cabbage
- 1 tsp Chinese Five Spice seasoning (see Glossary)
- 8 sheets thawed phyllo pastry

In a lightly oiled sauté pan, crumble tofu together with chicken style soup base and fry until golden brown. Sauté onion, carrot and celery separately in a lightly oiled frying pan until tender. Sauté the shredded cabbage in a small amount of oil until tender.

Add sautéed vegetables and Chinese Five Spice to tofu mixture and combine well. Chill mixture.

Preheat oven to 375° F

Place two sheets of phyllo pastry on counter top. Brush lightly with olive or grape seed oil. Put 1/2 cup of egg roll mixture along one edge of the pastry sheets and roll. Cut into 3 inch long pieces. This should yield about 4 egg rolls.

Repeat using remaining phyllo and filling. Place on a non-stick baking sheet, seam side down. Bake for 20 minutes or until golden brown.

Note: The egg rolls can be frozen prior to baking. Bake directly from freezer on a baking sheet at 375° F for 20-25 minutes.

Makes 16 egg rolls

Fire Hall Pasta

A delicious garlic pasta everyone will love.

- 1 1/2 cups broccoli florets
- 1/2 cup julienne cut carrots (optional)
- 1/2 lb. asparagus
- 1/3 cup olive oil
- 4-5 garlic cloves, minced
- 2 green onions, chopped
- sprinkle of hot red pepper flakes
- 1/2 cup whole grape tomatoes
- 1/2 can whole black olives
- 1/2 box (454 g) white linguine pasta
- 1/2 box (454 g) whole wheat linguine or spaghetti
- 1 Tbsp dried basil
- 1/2 tsp sea salt
- 1/4 cup soy parmesan for garnish
- 1/4 cup minced parsley

Steam broccoli, carrots and asparagus until al dente. Drop into a cold water bath. Drain. One half hour before mealtime, put on a large pot of water. Add salt and dried basil leaves to water. Bring to a boil.

Slowly heat olive oil in a small pot on medium low. Turn heat to low. Add garlic, onions and pepper flakes. Simmer for about 15 minutes (careful not to burn the garlic). Add tomatoes to the oil and cook until skins start to split. Remove the tomatoes and set them aside with the steamed broccoli, carrots and asparagus. Heat olives in the infused oil until ready to serve.

Put pasta in the pot of boiling seasoned water and cook for about 8 minutes. Do not overcook. Drain. If you have to keep the pasta warm, drizzle with a small amount of the infused oil, cover with tin foil, and hold in a 200° F oven. To serve, toss the seasoned oil and olives with the pasta. Arrange the steamed broccoli, carrots, asparagus and tomatoes on top of the pasta and sprinkle with soyparmesan and minced parsley.

Serves 6 - 8

Fish Sticks

- 2 cups water
- 1 cup quick oats
- 3 cups cottage cheese (see recipe page 117)
- 3/4 cup flaxseed gel (see recipe page 200)
- 1 cup multi-grain cracker crumbs
- 1 cup diced onions
- 2 Tbsp chicken style soup base
- 1/2 tsp salt

Cook oats in water for 5 minutes. In a large bowl, mix cottage cheese, flaxseed gel, cracker crumbs, onions and seasoning. Add cooked oatmeal and combine well.

Spread mixture evenly on cookie sheet lined with parchment paper. Bake at 275° F for 45 minutes. Refrigerate overnight to set mixture.

Slice mixture into 2 x 4 inch strips. (Freeze at this point, if you wish).
Dip sticks in Cornflake Breading (see recipe below), taking care to coat all sides thoroughly and evenly.

In a non-stick or lightly oiled fry pan, cook fish sticks slowly, over medium heat, until golden brown on both sides.

Serve hot with lemon wedges, tartar sauce, potato wedges or french fries.

Tip: If cornflake crumbs refuse to adhere, first dip quickly in soy milk and then in crumb mixture.

Cornflake Breading

- 2 cups finely crushed cornflakes
- 1 tsp onion powder
- salt to taste

Mix ingredients in a shallow bowl. Use as a breading for any recipes that require a breading mix.

Fried Tofu Cubes (Two Ways)

Use these tofu cubes in salads, over noodles or rice with curry sauce.

- 1-454 g package medium firm tofu
- 1/2 cup cornstarch
- 1 tsp paprika
- 1/4 tsp sea salt
- 1 tsp dried vegetable seasoning (see Glossary)
- 1/4 tsp fresh ground black pepper
- grape seed oil for frying

Rinse tofu and drain in a colander with a weight on top or overnight in its package with a towel to absorb moisture.

Mix cornstarch and seasonings in a shallow dish.

Cut tofu into bite size cubes and coat with the cornstarch, paprika, salt, dried vegetable seasoning and pepper mixture.

Heat oil in a skillet on medium high heat. Add tofu cubes and fry until golden brown. Do this in small batches to keep the oil temperature from dropping.
Drain tofu on paper towels.

Variation: Combine all ingredients and coat tofu. Cook tofu cubes as in recipe for fried tofu cubes

Serves 6

- 1 cup nutritional yeast
- 1/2 cup wheat germ
- 1 Tbsp garlic powder
- 1 tsp dried vegetable seasoning (see Glossary)
- 1/4 tsp sea salt
- 1/4 fresh ground black pepper
- 1 tsp paprika

Hungarian Potato Goulash

- olive oil – enough to sauté onion
- 1 large onion, diced (set aside 2 Tbsp)
- 1 1/2 tsp sweet Hungarian paprika
- 1/2 tsp hot Hungarian paprika
- 1-2 diced peppers, combination of yellow, green and red
- 1 medium tomato, seeded and diced
- 1-2 tsp chicken style soup base
- 6 average size potatoes, peeled and diced
- 1 cup of beef substitute (gluten or beef strips)
- 1 tsp sodium reduced soy sauce
- 1 Tbsp roux to thicken goulash (see Cooking Terms)

Roux

- 3 Tbsp olive oil
- 6 Tbsp flour

Sauté onion on medium heat until transparent. Add paprika. Add pepper and saute until peppers turn bright. Stir in tomato, diced potato, chicken soup base, and enough water to cover the potatoes. Bring to boil, reduce heat to medium, cook potatoes until tender. While potatoes are cooking, cut vegetarian strips into bite sized pieces. Add the remaining 2 Tbsp onion and soy sauce. Sauté in small amount of oil until brown. Add this to the goulash after potatoes are cooked.

To thicken goulash, remove some sauce from the goulash, whisk in the roux until blended.

Heat oil. Mix in flour and cook gently to golden brown, stirring constantly. Add 3 Tbsp of roux to liquid from goulash whisk this thickened paste back into the goulash; Cook for 5-10 minutes, or until sauce thickens. Use this roux to help thicken any gravy-type sauce. Refrigerate any unused portion.

Variation: You can leave the potatoes out and prepare them separately in your favourite way, serving the goulash over the potatoes. If you make the goulash this way, use 6 Tbsp. of the cooked roux to thicken the sauce. Goulash can also be served over noodles or grains.

Serves 4 - 6

Irish Stew

- 6 small potatoes
- 1 small turnip (optional)
- 2 medium carrots
- 2 stalks celery
- 1 medium onion, coarsely chopped
- 1 cup frozen or fresh peas
- 1 cup commercial gluten strips or Marinated Korean Gluten (see recipe page 207)
- 1 recipe Creamy Cashew or Light Vegetarian Gravy (see recipes page 109)

Peel potatoes and turnips. Cut into fairly large pieces, and parboil on high heat for about 10 minutes.

Peel carrot, chop carrot and celery into large pieces and parboil for about 5 minutes. Drain and set aside all parboiled vegetables.

Sauté onion in a lightly oiled pan until tender.

Arrange marinated gluten, parboiled vegetables and fried onions in an oiled casserole dish. Add peas. Pour prepared gravy over top, cover and bake at 350° F for 40 minutes. If your gravy is too thin, make a paste with the gravy and a roux (see Hungarian Goulash recipe page 205) and return to stew pot to thicken.

You can also use this stew as pot pie filler, using Basic Pie Crust recipe as a topping.

Serves 4

Korean Gluten

Gluten, also known as seitan, is commercially available. This is a homemade recipe if you have time and want to save on cost.

- 1/3 cup dried soy beans
- 2/3 cup walnuts
- 1 Tbsp garlic powder or 3 crushed garlic cloves
- 1 large onion, chopped
- 2 cups water
- 3 cups gluten flour
- 3/4 cup unbleached white flour
- 1 tsp olive oil

Place soy beans in enough water to cover and let soak overnight.
Drain, add fresh water and boil in a small pot for 15 minutes to make them easier for blending.

Place partially cooked soy beans, plus walnuts, garlic and onion in a blender. Add 2 cups water and blend until smooth.

In a large bowl, combine gluten flour and unbleached flour. Pour in blended soy bean mixture and mix quickly to make dough.

Form dough into 8 large patties about 3/4 inch thick.

Add olive oil to fry pan and brown patties on both sides. At this point you can freeze the patties to use in future recipes.

One patty will yield about 1 1/4 cups of gluten strips. These strips are in the "raw state" and will have to be fried and marinated for use in recipes that call for beef (see Korean Gluten Marinade recipe page 208).

Yields approximately 10 cups of strips

Korean Gluten Marinade

- 2 frozen patties or 2 cups Gluten Strips (see recipe page 207)
- 1 clove crushed garlic
- 1/3 cup sodium reduced soy sauce
- 1/3 cup water
- 1/4 cup chopped onion and/or green pepper

While still slightly frozen, cut the patties into very thin strips and fry again on both sides in a lightly oiled non-stick pan.

Combine garlic, soy sauce, water and onion or green pepper in a bowl. Add gluten strips and marinate for one hour. If you prefer a stronger flavour, allow gluten to marinate longer.

Place strips and marinade into a pan and simmer until liquid is absorbed.

The gluten strips are now ready to be used in recipes. Marinated gluten strips can be ground up and used in place of hamburger in stroganoff, chilli, cabbage roll or lasagne recipes, and used in stir fries.

Lasagne

- 12 large lasagne noodles cooked al dente
- 1-454 g package medium tofu, rinsed and drained
- 1 1/2 Tbsp chicken style soup base
- 1/2 tsp dried vegetable garlic seasoning (see Glossary)
- 1/2 cup parmesan cheese
- 1 1/2 cup soya mozzarella grated
- 3 cups spinach, cleaned, with stems removed
- 1 recipe of spaghetti sauce with burger crumble (see Glossary)

Makes one 9 x 13 inch pan
Sauté tofu in a little olive oil with the chicken style soup base and vegetable seasonings until nicely browned. Set aside in bowl.
In oiled 9 x 13 inch pan, layer as follows:
1 cup of spaghetti sauce to cover bottom
3 lasagne noodles
1 cup of spaghetti sauce, 1/2 cup grated mozzarella
3 lasagne noodles cut to fit pan and crisscrossed in opposite direction
Spread fried tofu and chopped spinach evenly over next layer, plus
1/4 cup parmesan cheese
3 lasagne noodles
1 cup spaghetti sauce, 1/2 cup grated mozzarella
3 lasagne noodles cut to fit pan and crisscrossed in opposite direction
Cover the final layer with 1 cup of spaghetti sauce. Sprinkle with remaining 1/4 cup parmesan and 1/2 cup grated mozzarella cheese.
Cover and bake 1 hour at 350° F.
Uncover and bake 10-15 minutes until golden brown on top.
Remove from oven and let stand for 10 minutes before serving.

Serves 6 - 8

Lazy Perogies

- 2 cups cooked favourite noodles
- 2 cups well seasoned mashed potatoes
- 1 recipe tofu cottage cheese (see recipe, page 117)
- 2 cups grated soy cheddar cheese
- 2 Tbsp olive oil
- 1 cup onion, chopped
- 1 tsp dried vegetable garlic seasoning

Mix mashed potatoes and cottage cheese together.
Sauté onion in olive oil until golden brown. Season with garlic seasoning.

Oil a 9 x 13 inch pan. Line with half of noodles.

Spread with the mashed potato mixture and cottage cheese. Add the other half of noodles.

Top with soy cheddar cheese. Saute onion in a little olive oil and spread on top. Cover with foil and bake at 350° F for 30 minutes or until golden.

Let mixture cool for 10 minutes after removing from oven.
Serve with soy sour cream, garnished with fresh dill.

Serves 6

Pasta Primavera

- 3 cups cooked, drained multi-coloured rotini pasta
- 1 Tbsp olive oil
- 1-2 cloves fresh minced garlic
- 1 tsp garlic plus seasoning
- 1/2 tsp dried vegetable seasoning (see Glossary)
- 1 Tbsp chicken style soup base (see Glossary)
- 1 Tbsp canned capers, coarsely chopped
- 1 medium tomato, diced fine
- 2 Tbsp dried basil or 4 Tbsp fresh basil, chiffonade cut (see Cooking Terms)
- salt to taste

Heat olive oil, garlic and seasonings in frying pan on medium-low heat. Add cooked pasta and toss until evenly coated with oil and seasonings. Continue to toss until pasta is heated. Add capers and tomatoes and toss for one minute.

Garnish with soy parmesan cheese and fresh basil.

Variation: A combination of your favourite veggies can be stir fried along with seasonings, such as diced canned artichoke hearts, grilled red, green or yellow peppers, carrots, celery, mushrooms, olives, broccoli.

Boiled Brown Rice

If you don't have a rice cooker, here is a method that cooks the rice perfectly.

- 1 1/2 cups basmati brown rice (long or short grain)
- 3 cups cold water
- 1/2 tsp salt

Wash the rice in several changes of water and drain thoroughly.

Put the rice in a heavy 1 1/2 L pot. Add 3 cups of water and leave it to soak for 1 hour. Add salt and bring to a boil. Cover, turn heat to very low, and cook for 35 minutes. Turn the heat off and let the rice sit covered and undisturbed for 10 minutes. Fluff rice gently with a fork and serve.

Refrigerate overnight and break apart the grains for use in fried rice recipes.

Serves 4

Firehall Pasta

Chinese Fried Rice

- 4 cups cooked basmati brown rice (day-old)
- 1 Tbsp sesame oil
- $1/2$ cup finely diced carrot
- $1/2$ cup finely diced celery
- $1/2$ cup sliced green onion
- 1 tsp Chinese Five Spice seasoning (optional)
- 2 Tbsp sodium reduced soy sauce
- $1/2$ cup green peas
- 1 Tbsp vegetarian chicken seasoning
- $1/4$ cup roasted sesame seeds (optional)

Heat sesame oil in sauté pan or wok over medium heat. Add carrot, celery, onion and sauté for several minutes. Add Chinese Five Spice, soy sauce, rice peas and vegetarian chicken seasoning. Sauté until rice is heated. Garnish with toasted sesame seeds.

Serves 4 - 6

East Indian Fried Rice

- 4 cups cooked basmati brown rice (day-old)
- 1 Tbsp olive oil
- 1 onion diced
- 1/2 tsp garam masala
- 1 tsp freshly grated ginger
- 1 tsp turmeric
- 1 cup green peas, fresh or frozen
- 1/4 cup vegetarian chicken broth
- 1/4 cup almonds, slivered and toasted
- 1/4 cup cashews, coarsely chopped and toasted

Heat olive oil over medium heat. Sauté onion for several minutes. Add garam masala, ginger and turmeric. Add rice, stir to coat each kernel with seasoned oil. Cover the pan with a tight fitting lid. If the rice seems dry, add some chicken broth. Add the uncooked peas and cook until peas are tender and bright green.

Serve garnished with toasted almonds and cashews.

Serves 4 - 6

Greek Fried Rice

- 4 cups cooked brown basmati rice (day-old)
- 1 Tbsp olive oil
- 1/2 cup diced red pepper
- 1/2 cup diced green pepper
- 1/2 cup chopped green onion
- 1/2 Tbsp dried oregano
- 1/2 cup chopped parsley
- 1/2 cup chopped Kalamata olives
- 1 Tbsp vegetarian chicken seasoning
- 1/2 cup pine nuts, roasted (optional)

Heat olive oil in sauté pan over medium heat. Sauté peppers and onion for several minutes. Add rice and seasonings. Sauté until rice is heated. Add parsley and olives. Garnish with chopped roasted pine nuts.

Serves 6 - 8

Mexican Fried Rice

- 4 cups cooked basmati brown rice (day-old)
- 1 Tbsp olive oil
- 1/2 cup diced celery
- 1/2 cup diced red pepper
- 1/2 cup diced green onion
- 1/2 cup kernel corn (fresh or frozen)
- 1/2 cup tomato salsa (fresh or commercial)
- 1/2 tsp smoked paprika
- dash cayenne
- 1/4 tsp celery salt
- 1/4 cup chopped cilantro or parsley

Heat olive oil over medium heat. Sauté celery, red pepper, green onion and corn for several minutes. Add rice, salsa, paprika, cayenne and celery salt. Stir fry until rice is heated through. Garnish with cilantro or parsley.

Serves 4 - 6

Shepherd's Pie

- 1 Tbsp olive oil
- 1 cup onion, minced
- 1 cup carrot, minced
- 1 cup celery, minced
- 1/4 cup red pepper, minced
- 2 cloves minced garlic
- 2 cups (312 g package) veggie ground (see Glossary)
- 2 cups light Veggie Beef Gravy (see recipe page 109)
- 2 cups kernel corn, fresh or frozen
- 1 cup fresh or frozen peas
- 4 cups seasoned whipped potatoes
- 2 Tbsp melted non-dairy butter
- paprika to garnish

Heat olive oil in sauté pan. Sauté onion, carrot, celery, red pepper and garlic until onion becomes translucent. Add crumbled veggie ground and gravy. Simmer on low for 15 minutes. Transfer mixture to a 9 cup (2.8 litre) casserole dish. Top with corn and peas. Cover with whipped potatoes and drizzle with non-dairy butter. Sprinkle with paprika.

Bake at 375° F for 30-40 minutes or until potatoes are golden.

Rest casserole for 15 minutes before serving.

Variation: Make a chicken flavoured Shepherd's Pie by using veggie ground chicken and light vegetarian chicken gravy.

Serves 6 - 8

Spaghetti Sauce

- 3 Tbsp olive oil
- 1 medium onion, diced
- 1 bell pepper, diced
- 3 garlic cloves, minced
- 1-28 fl oz (796 ml) can diced Roma tomatoes
- 1-5.5 oz can tomato paste
- 1 cup V8 juice
- 1 can tomato soup
- 1 tsp dried garlic vegetable seasoning
- 1/8 tsp red pepper flakes (to taste)
- dash of cayenne
- 2 tsp dried basil (or use more if fresh)
- 1/4 cup red wine (optional)
- 2 Tbsp sun-dried tomatoes, oil packed
- 1 Tbsp maple syrup or organic cane sugar
- 1/4 cup soy parmesan for garnish

Sauté onion in olive oil over medium heat until translucent. Add bell pepper and garlic, sauté for several minutes. Add remaining ingredients.
Bring to a boil, reduce heat and simmer for an hour or more. Serve over cooked spaghetti or linguine noodles. Garnish with soy parmesan.

Make this sauce ahead of time and refrigerate. Use in lasagne, for tofu croquettes and tofu manicotti.

If you prefer a meaty type of sauce, add 2 cups (312 g package) of veggie ground (see Glossary) during simmering time.

Makes 5 cups

Spicy Chili

- 1 Tbsp olive oil
- 1 cup chopped onion
- 1 clove garlic, chopped
- 1 small jalapeno pepper, diced fine
- 1 tsp ground cumin
- 1 tsp chilli powder
- 1/8 tsp cayenne
- 1 cup chopped celery
- 1 cup chopped green pepper
- 2 cups tomato juice
- 2 cups canned tomatoes
- 1-5.5 oz can tomato paste
- 1 Tbsp organic cane sugar
- 1- 19 oz can kidney beans
- 2 cups (312 g package) veggie ground (see Glossary)

Heat olive oil in a large saucepan and sauté onion, garlic, jalapeno, cumin, chilli powder and cayenne for several minutes.

Add celery and peppers and sauté for several minutes. Pour in tomato juice and canned tomatoes, tomato paste, sugar and kidney beans and slowly bring to a boil. Reduce heat to medium low. Crumble in veggie ground.
Simmer slowly for 1 hour, stirring to prevent scorching. Taste and adjust seasoning prior to serving.

Serves 8

Tofu Croquettes

- 1/3 cup minced onion
- 1 Tbsp olive oil
- 1/2-454 g package medium tofu
- 1 1/2 cups soft whole wheat bread crumbs
- 1/2 cup finely ground walnuts
- 1 Tbsp chicken style soup base
- 1 Tbsp nutritional yeast flakes
- 1/2 tsp dried ground sage
- 1/2 tsp salt

Sauté onion in olive oil until soft. Drain and rinse tofu, add to blender and process until smooth.

Add blended tofu, sautéed onions and all remaining ingredients in a bowl and combine well. Place mixture in refrigerator and allow to chill for at least 1 hour.

Use a 1/4 cup ice cream scoop to form mixture into croquette balls. Place croquettes on an oiled baking dish. Bake at 350° F for 20-30 minutes or until brown.

Before serving, cover the baked croquettes with your favourite gravy or spaghetti sauce and bake 350° F for another 15-20 minutes.

Tip: Tofu croquettes freeze well. Prepare ahead, and then thaw only the amount you need for your meal.

Makes 8-10 1/2 cup croquettes

Tofu Manicotti

- 1 cup onion, minced
- 1 cup celery, minced
- 2 cloves garlic, minced
- 1/2 sweet red pepper, minced
- 1-454 g package medium tofu
- 3 Tbsp chicken style soup base
- 1 Tbsp dried vegetable seasoning (see Glossary)
- 1-300 g package frozen spinach thawed
- 1-225 g package manicotti pasta
- 2 cups Spaghetti Sauce (see recipe page 219)
- 1/2 cup soy mozzarella grated
- 1/4 cup soy parmesan, grated

Sauté onions, celery, garlic and red pepper until tender.

Drain tofu, rinse and pat dry. Mash into frying pan with sautéed vegetables, chicken soup base and vegetable seasoning. Sauté until most of the moisture has cooked out of the tofu. Add chopped spinach which has been squeezed dry and combine well with tofu mixture. Cool slightly.

Meanwhile, cook manicotti al dente according to package directions. Drain but do not rinse the pasta. Spoon a layer of tomato sauce in the bottom of a 9 x 13 inch pan.

Fill the pasta tubes with the tofu filling (a pastry bag or ziploc bag with tip cut from one corner works well for this). Place all the filled pasta in the baking pan. Pour over more tomato sauce. Cover, bake for 45 minutes at 350° F. Uncover, sprinkle with cheese and return to oven until cheese melts.

Variation: You can use Tofu Cottage Cheese (see recipe page 117) for filling instead.

Note: 1/2 package (225 g) manicotti shells makes 7 manicotti. Double filling recipe to use the whole package.

Makes 7 manicottis

Walnut Burgers

The burger crumble and walnuts make this a "beef" type of burger.

- 1/2 cup diced onion
- 1 cup fresh whole wheat bread crumbs
- 1 cup cooked brown rice
- 2/3 cup ground walnuts
- 1/2 cup finely chopped celery
- 1/2 cup quick oats, uncooked
- 1 tsp dried parsley flakes
- 1/4 cup raw cashew pieces
- 2 Tbsp sodium reduced soy sauce
- 1/2 cup medium tofu, drained
- 1/4 cup water as needed
- 1 Tbsp gluten or garbanzo flour
- 1/2 tsp salt
- 1/2 cup soy cheddar cheese grated
- 1 cup veggie ground (see Glossary)

Sauté onions in a non-stick or lightly oiled pan.

In a large bowl, combine onions, breadcrumbs, rice, walnuts, celery, oats and parsley. Mix well then set aside.

Pour cashews, soy sauce and tofu into a blender along with enough water to blend until creamy and smooth.

Add gluten flour and salt. Pulse the blender for several seconds.

Mix blended liquid with bread crumb mixture.

Add cheese and burger crumble. Mix until well combined.

See tips for making veggie burgers (Glossary).

Serves 8 - 10

Walnut Burgers with Apricot

Dried apricots give this burger a hint of sweetness.

- 1 medium onion, diced
- 1 medium red pepper, diced
- 2 tsp vegetarian beef flavoured soup base
- 1/2 -454 g package medium tofu, drained
- 15 dried apricots, minced
- 1/2 cup fresh parsley, minced
- 2 Tbsp sodium reduced soy sauce
- 2 Tbsp Dijon mustard
- 1/2 tsp garlic powder
- 1/2 cup finely chopped walnuts
- 1 cup raw quick cooking oats
- 1/2 cup fresh bread crumbs

Rinse and drain tofu. Wrap in cloth and return to package. Refrigerate.
If pressed for time, cut tofu cube in half, wrap in cloth, place in colander with weight on top for 30 minutes.

Sauté the diced onion. Add the red peppers and beef flavoured soup base.

With a fork break apart tofu and mash into the onion mixture. Combine with apricots, parsley, soy sauce, Dijon mustard, garlic powder, walnuts, oats, and bread crumbs. Refrigerate overnight.

Cook over medium heat in lightly oiled pan. Turn when bottom is browned.

See tips for making veggie burgers (see Glossary).

Serves 8-10

Notes:

Desserts

Desserts

Glazed Fresh Fruit Tart

Egg Substitutes

Baking with eggs does several important things. They bind ingredients, help with rising and provide extra liquid.

Here are several substitutes to use when eggs are called for in a recipe.

Tofu: Use about $1/4$ cup dessert tofu, mashed, to replace 1 egg.

Powdered egg replacer: Contains potato starch, tapioca flour and leavening agents. Blend the powder with water to replace the egg. Available in health food stores.

Flaxseed Gel

- 2 cups water
- 6 Tbsp flaxseed

In a pot, add flaxseed and water, bring to a boil. As soon as it begins to boil, it will turn from a watery liquid to a jelly-like consistency. Remove pot from stove and immediately pour the mixture through a strainer and into a container.
Cool and store in refrigerator. Will keep 5 days refrigerated. Use as an egg white replacer or binding agent

$1/4$ cup flaxseed gel = 1 egg

Ambrosia

So good for so many reasons.

- 1-398 ml can of coconut milk
- 1/4 cup frozen pineapple juice concentrate
- 1/3 cup minute tapioca
- 3 Tbsp honey
- 1/2 cup unsweetened desiccated coconut
- 1 tsp vanilla
- 1-398 ml can crushed pineapple, drained
- 1-284 ml can unsweetened mandarin orange sections, drained
- 2 cups red seedless grapes, halved
- Whipped Coconut Cream (see recipe page 253)
- 3/4 cup coconut (toasted in dry frying pan)

Combine coconut milk, frozen pineapple juice, tapioca and honey, and bring to a full boil in a saucepan over medium heat. Stir constantly.

Let this mixture cool. Then add unsweetened desiccated coconut, vanilla, crushed pineapple, unsweetened mandarin orange sections, red seedless grapes, whipped coconut cream and coconut.

Add all ingredients together. Mix well and then fold in 1 recipe of Whipped Coconut Cream. Serve chilled. Garnish with toasted coconut.

Serves 6 - 8

Apple Strudel

Gingersnaps add a hint of spice to this strudel.

- 6 apples (Granny Smith, Spartan combination)
- 1/4 cup dark raisins
- 1/3 cup organic cane sugar
- 1 Tbsp corn starch dissolved in 1 Tbsp water
- 1/2 tsp cinnamon
- 1/2 tsp vanilla
- 1/2 cup walnuts
- 4 Gingersnap cookies (see recipe page 242)
- 1/4 cup melted non-dairy butter (see Glossary)
- 6 sheets phyllo dough

To prepare filling: Sauté apples in 1/3 cup water. Add raisins, sugar and cinnamon. Add cornstarch mixture. Cook, stirring occasionally until apples are tender. Add vanilla. Cool completely. In a food processor, combine the walnuts and Gingersnaps to make crumbs.
Preheat oven to 375° F and spray a baking sheet with cooking spray.

To assemble strudel: Reserve 2 tsp of non-dairy butter. Place a sheet of phyllo dough on a piece of parchment paper that has been cut slightly larger than the phyllo sheet. Lightly brush phyllo with butter. Add another phyllo sheet. Sprinkle with 1 Tbsp of crumb mixture. Repeat, using all six phyllo sheets, butter and crumb mixture. End with the phyllo.

Spoon apples over the phyllo, leaving a 1 inch border around the phyllo. Lift one long end of the parchment and fold the strudel, jelly roll style. Place seam side down on the prepared baking sheet. Brush with remaining non-dairy butter.

Tip: Making sure not to go through to filling, lightly score the top layer of phyllo for easier slicing.
Bake at 375° for 25-30 minutes, or until golden.

Serves 6 - 8

Apple Turnovers

Filling:

- 3 Granny Smith apples
- 2 Tbsp organic cane sugar
- 2 Tbsp grape seed oil
- cinnamon to taste

Peel, core and slice the apples. Place apples and sugar in a heated frying pan and stir-fry until lightly caramelized. Remove from heat. Add cinnamon. Chill well.

Pastry: Make a recipe of Basic Pie Crust (see recipe page 232)
Cut off pieces the size of walnuts and roll out into a circle. Place a spoonful of apple filling in the centre and fold dough over. Crimp the edges with a fork and remove any excess dough. Bake on an oiled baking sheet at 375° F for 25 minutes or until golden brown.

Basic Pie Crust

- 1/2 cup whole wheat flour
- 1 1/2 cups unbleached white flour
- 1/2 cup grape seed oil or non-dairy butter, melted
- 1/2 tsp salt
- 3 Tbsp organic cane sugar
- 1/2 tsp baking powder
- 1/2 cup+ cold water

Mix dry ingredients together. Add oil or non-dairy butter and rub with fingers until the mixture is mealy. Add cold water (start with half a cup of cold water), mix lightly to a pastry consistency (careful not to over mix, or the dough will become tough). Divide dough in half. Roll out on wax paper 2 inches larger than pan dimensions. Ease the dough into the pan, patting it lightly against the bottom and sides of the pan to prevent air pockets. Trim the excess dough on lip of pan with a knife. Make a decorative edge with a fork or your fingers.

If baking unfilled, poke holes in the dough generously with a fork. Bake at 400°F for 10-12 minutes or until lightly browned.

For baked filled pies, follow recipe directions.

Black Bottom Cupcakes

- 1 cup soy cream cheese
- 1/3 cup dry sweetener of choice
- 1/8 tsp salt
- 1 cup miniature semisweet vegan chocolate chips
- 1 1/2 cups all-purpose flour
- 2/3 cup dry sweetener of choice
- 1/4 cup unsweetened cocoa powder
- 1 tsp baking soda
- 1/2 tsp salt
- 1 cup water
- 1/3 cup vegetable oil
- 1 Tbsp apple cider vinegar
- 1 tsp vanilla extract

Preheat oven to 350° F.

Line muffin tins with paper cups or spray lightly with non-stick cooking spray.

In a medium bowl, beat the cream cheese, 1/3 cup sweetener and 1/8 tsp salt until light and fluffy. Stir in the chocolate chips and set aside.

In a large bowl, mix together the flour, 2/3 cup sweetener, cocoa, baking soda and salt. Make a well in the centre and add the water, oil, vinegar and vanilla. Stir until well blended.

Fill muffin tins 1/3 full with the batter and top with a tablespoon of cream cheese mixture.

Bake 25-30 minutes.

Makes 12 cupcakes

Black Forest Parfait

- 1 recipe of Chocolate Cake
  (see recipe page 237)
- 1 recipe of Chocolate Mousse
  (see recipe page 238)
- 1 recipe of Whipped Coconut Cream
  (see recipe page 253)
- 3 cups fresh or frozen cherries, pitted and halved mixed with 1 Tbsp sweetener of choice

If using frozen cherries, remove from freezer and thaw.
Make Chocolate Cake, cool completely, cut into cubes.

Make Chocolate Mousse, refrigerate.

Whip Coconut Cream, refrigerate. For a large crowd, use a decorative glass bowl. If making individual servings, tall glasses or stemmed glasses make a pretty presentation.

Assembly:
First layer – Whipped Coconut Cream
Second layer – cherries
Third layer – cubed Chocolate Cake
Fourth layer – Chocolate Mousse
Repeat layers ending with Whipped Coconut Cream.
Top with a cherry.

Note: You will probably have leftover cake from this recipe.

Blueberry Kuchen

- 2 cups unbleached white flour
- 3/4 tsp salt
- 1/2 cup organic cane sugar
- 1 tsp baking powder
- 1/2 cup non-dairy butter
- 2 cups frozen or fresh unsweetened blueberries (may substitute with fresh sweetened raspberries or pitted cherries)

Preheat oven to 350° F.

In a large bowl combine flour, salt, organic cane sugar and baking powder. Knead in non-dairy butter until mixture sticks together. Press 2/3 of crumb mixture in the bottom of an 8 x 8 inch pan. Cover crust with blueberries. Sprinkle remaining 1/3 of crumb mixture over blueberries.

Bake for 30 minutes until golden brown. Serve with Pear Cream or Whipped Coconut Cream. (see recipes pages 113, 253)

Serves 6

Chocolate Chip Cookies

By changing a few ingredients, this recipe can be changed into a bar or spice cookie.

- 1/2 cup non-dairy butter
- 2/3 cup organic cane sugar
- 1/2 cup dessert tofu
- 1/4 cup tofu milk (or milk of choice)
- 2 tsp vanilla
- 1/2 cup unbleached flour
- 1/2 tsp baking powder
- 1/2 tsp baking soda
- 1/2 tsp salt
- 1-2 cups quick cooking oats
- 1 cup vegan chocolate chips or carob chips
- 1/2 cup chopped walnuts

Cream butter and sugar. Add tofu, tofu milk and vanilla. Stir in flour, baking powder, baking soda and salt. Add enough oats to make a drop cookie consistency. Stir in chips and walnuts.

Drop cookie dough by tablespoon on oiled baking sheet or parchment lined baking sheet. Bake at 350° F until golden brown (about 10 minutes).

To make a bar: Pat dough into an oiled 9 x 13 inch cake pan and bake at 350° F for about 25 minutes. Remove from oven and cut into bar sized pieces.

To make a spice cookie: Add 1/2 cup raisins, 1/2 tsp cinnamon and 1/4 tsp ground cloves. Omit chocolate chips.

Makes about 2 dozen cookies

Chocolate Cake

- 1 1/2 cups unbleached flour
- 3/4 cup dry sweetener of choice
- 1/2 cup cocoa powder
- 2 tsp cinnamon (optional)
- 1/4 tsp salt
- 1 tsp baking soda
- 1 cup cold water
- 1/4 cup grapeseed oil
- 1 Tbsp apple cider vinegar
- 1 Tbsp vanilla

Preheat oven to 350° F.

In a bowl, sift together flour, sweetener, cocoa, cinnamon, salt and baking soda. Make a well in sifted ingredients. Add water, oil, vinegar and vanilla. Stir just until mixture comes together.

Pour batter into an oiled 8 x 12 inch cake pan. Level batter out with a spatula. Bake 20-25 minutes or until a toothpick inserted in center comes out clean. Remove from oven and cool on cooling rack.

Note: Adding 1/2 cup chopped pecans or walnuts to the batter turns this cake into a brownie.

Chocolate Ganache Icing

- 1 cup semi-sweet chocolate chips
- 2 Tbsp non-dairy butter
- 1 Tbsp honey or maple syrup

Melt chocolate chips in a double boiler. Stir in non-dairy butter and honey or maple syrup as soon as chocolate chips have melted. Stir until mixture is smooth. This icing will thicken at room temperature and hardens quickly if refrigerated.

Makes 1 1/2 cups

Chocolate Mousse

This mousse is easy to make. Tofu replaces the eggs and heavy cream used in traditional mousse recipes.

- 1 package (350 g) dessert tofu
- 3/4 cup semi-sweet vegan chocolate chips

Empty contents of dessert tofu into a blender. Melt chocolate chips over double boiler. Add melted chocolate chips with the tofu and puree. Pour into dessert bowls and refrigerate until set (about 40 minutes) Lasts for several days refrigerated.

Top with Whipped Coconut Cream (see recipe page 253). Use as a dip for strawberries, or try the Black Forest Parfait (see recipe page 234).

Serves 6

Coconut Berry Fool

So easy to make and so good!

- 4 cups partially frozen strawberries, raspberries or blackberries
- 1 can coconut milk, well chilled (use a product with 12 g fat content)
- 1 Tbsp dry sweetener of choice
- 1 tsp vanilla

Break apart partially frozen berries. Remove coconut milk from fridge and whip it with sweetener and vanilla. Fold the berries into the coconut milk. The more frozen the berries are, the stiffer the dessert. If you want a pudding consistency, use completely defrosted or fresh, mashed berries. If mixture is too soft, place in the freezer.

Serve topped with fresh berries.

Serves 6

Black Forest Parfait

Coconut Pie Crust

- 1 1/2 cups coconut (finely ground)
- 1 Tbsp unbleached white flour
- 1/4 cup tofu milk (or milk of choice)

Preheat oven to 350° F.

Mix coconut and flour together in a small bowl. Pour in milk and mix.
Pat crumb mixture evenly over the bottom of a lightly oiled, 8 inch pie plate or 8 x 8 inch cake pan.
Bake for 10 minutes or until the edges just begin to turn golden brown.
Cool and add filling.

Makes one 8 inch pie crust

Date Filled Cookies

This recipe can be turned into a date square.

Date Filling

- 2 cups finely chopped dates
- 1 cup water
- 1 Tbsp sugar
- 2 Tbsp lemon juice

Cookie Dough

- 2 cups flour
- 1 1/2 tsp baking soda
- 1/2 tsp salt
- 1 1/2 cups organic cane sugar
- 6 cups quick cooking rolled oats
- 1 cup vegetable oil
- 1 cup cold water

To make filling, combine all ingredients in a saucepan and cook over medium heat until dates are soft and spreadable. Stir constantly then remove from heat and cool.

To make cookies, preheat oven to 350° F, mix together flour, baking soda and salt. Add sugar, oats, and oil. Combine well with fork, sprinkling with water, and mixing to make a soft (not sticky) dough. Roll dough very thin. Cut out 2 inch circles with floured cookie cutter. Bake 5-7 minutes on lightly oiled baking sheet. Cool. Spread cooled date filling on half cookie. Place other cookie halves on top to form sandwiches.

Makes about 24 cookies.

Tip: This recipe can be used as a date square also. Make 1 1/2 times more date mix for the amount of crumb dough. Use 3/4 cup water for the dough making a coarse crumb mixture. Press half the crumb mixture in an oiled 9 x 13 inch pan. Top with date mixture, then sprinkle with remaining crumb mixture. Bake at 350° for 35-40 minutes.

Makes a 9 x 13 inch pan.

Gingersnaps

Snappy and spicy. Use these tasty cookies in the Apple Strudel recipe.

- 2 1/4 cups all-purpose flour
- 2 tsp baking soda
- 1 tsp ground ginger
- 1 tsp ground cinnamon
- 1/2 tsp ground cloves
- 1/4 tsp salt
- 1 cup organic cane sugar
- 3/4 cup non-dairy butter or grape seed oil
- 1/4 cup molasses
- 1/4 cup dessert tofu
- sugar or dry sweetener of choice for dusting cookie (optional)

Stir together flour, baking soda, ginger, cinnamon, cloves, and salt. In a large mixing bowl. Combine sugar, oil or non-dairy butter, molasses, and tofu. Beat well. Combine dry and wet ingredients. Mix well.

Shape the dough into 1 inch balls. Roll in sugar, if desired. Flatten with bottom of a glass and pierce with fork. Place 2 inches apart on a dry baking sheet.

Bake in a 375° F oven about 10 minutes or until done.

Makes about 36 cookies

Glazed Fresh Fruit Tart

This pie is bursting with fresh fruit flavour.

- Make one Walnut Pie Crust (see recipe page 253)
- 6 cups sliced fresh peaches, nectarines, apricots or strawberries
- 1/2-2/3 cup dry sweetener of choice
- 3 Tbsp cornstarch
- 1/4 cup water
- 2 Tbsp lemon juice

Puree 2 cups fruit in a food processer. In a saucepan combine sugar and cornstarch. Stir in water, lemon juice and blended fruit. Cook over medium heat, stirring constantly until the cornstarch is clear and cooked. Pour over 4 cups of sliced fruit. Spoon fruit mixture into baked crust. Refrigerate for several hours or until set. Decorate with Whipped Coconut Cream or softened soy ice cream. Garnish with fruit slices.

Hedge Hogs

Soft and chewy and so easy to make!

- 2 Tbsp non-dairy butter
- 1 cup organic cane sugar
- 2 cups walnuts or pecans, chopped
- 2 cups dates, chopped
- 1/2 cup unbleached flour
- 2 tsp vanilla
- 1/2 package or 150 g dessert tofu
- 2-3 cups fancy long shredded coconut for coating

Measure all ingredients into a bowl (except for coconut) Mix well. Scoop a small amount (approximately 1 1/2 Tbsp) of mixture and shape into balls. Roll balls in coconut and place on an oiled baking sheet. Bake at 350° F for 12 minutes or until golden brown.

Makes 40 cookies

Lemon Pineapple Cheesecake

- 1 Walnut Pie Crust (see recipe page 253)
- 2 Tbsp unflavoured vegetable gelatin (see Glossary)
- 1 package lemon flavoured gelatin (see Glossary)
- 3/4 cup pineapple juice, from drained pineapple
- 1 cup pineapple juice, boiled
- 1 cup raw cashews
- 1/3 cup honey or sweetener of choice
- 3 Tbsp fresh lemon juice
- 1/2 tsp salt
- 6 ice cubes
- 1 cup soy cream cheese
- 1-10 oz can crushed pineapple drained (use the juice to soak gelatin)

Prepare Walnut Pie Crust. Place gelatin and cold pineapple juice into blender. Let soak a couple minutes. Pour boiled pineapple juice over soaked mixture and blend to dissolve gelatin.

Add cashews and blend until creamy and smooth. Add sweetener, lemon juice, salt, ice cubes and cream cheese and blend until smooth.

Pour into a bowl. Fold in crushed pineapple. Let set for one hour. Pour into a baked, cooled crust. Chill overnight. Decorate with fresh fruit.

Serves 6 - 8

Mango Pudding

A refreshing way to finish a meal.

- 1 can (30 oz or 750 ml) mango pulp
- 3 Tbsp fresh lemon juice
- 1 cup soy cream cheese
- 2 tsp instant clear gel (see Glossary)
- 2 ripe mangos chopped into bite-size pieces
- 1/4 cup dry sweetener of choice (optional)

Place first four ingredients in blender and blend until smooth. Add clear gel a teaspoon at a time and blend until desired thickness is obtained. Add sweetner if needed. Put into bowl and stir in the chopped fresh mango. Chill and serve topped with Whipped Coconut Cream (see recipe page 253).

Serves 4 - 6

Nettie's Coconut Cream Pie

- 3 cups hot water
- 3/4 cup dried pineapple pieces
- 1/3 cup tofu milk powder
- 1/2 cup cornstarch (scant)
- pinch of salt
- 1/2 tsp vanilla
- 1/2 tsp coconut flavouring

Soak pineapple in hot water, until water cools. Add to a blender with tofu milk powder, cornstarch and salt. Blend until smooth.
Pour blended mixture into a saucepan. Stir constantly over a medium heat until sauce thickens. Remove from heat and stir in vanilla and coconut flavouring.
Pour into a baked Coconut Pie Crust (see recipe page 240) or other pre-baked pie crust. Chill and serve.

Tip: To make a vanilla pie filling, simply omit the coconut flavouring.

Makes one 8 inch pie

Pear Coconut Pie

Serve this tasty pie with Whipped Coconut Cream or soy ice cream.

- One Walnut or Almond Pie Crust recipe in 10 inch spring form pan (see recipes page 253)
- 1/2 cup flour
- 3/4 cup shredded coconut
- 3/4 cup organic cane sugar
- 1/3 cup non-dairy butter
- 6 - 8 fresh pear halves, peeled and cored
- cinnamon to taste

Combine flour, coconut, organic cane sugar and non-dairy butter.
Rub together until crumbly. Sprinkle half this mixture over the pie crust.
Arrange the pear halves cut side down over the mixture.
Sprinkle with cinnamon and top with the remaining coconut mixture.

Bake at 425° F for 10 minutes. Reduce heat to 350° F and bake for 20 minutes, or until golden brown.

Pecan Squares

- 1/4 cup organic cane sugar
- 1/2 cup maple syrup
- 2 tsp vanilla
- 1/8 tsp salt
- 4 Tbsp vegan chocolate chips (or carob chips)
- 3 Tbsp non-dairy butter
- 1 1/2 cups chopped pecans
- 1/2 cup unbleached flour

Place sugar and syrup into a saucepan and bring to boil. Remove from heat and add vanilla, salt, chocolate chips and butter. Stir in pecans and flour. Press into 8 x 8 inch pan lined with parchment paper. Bake at 350° F for 25 minutes. Cut while warm. Remove squares from pan while still warm.

Mango Pudding, Hedgehogs, Sesame Fingers

Pumpkin Delight

- 1 recipe baked nut or crumb crust (see recipe page 253)
- 3 Tbsp unflavoured vegetable gelatin (see Glossary)
- $3/4$ cup water
- 1 cup boiling water
- $1/2$ cup organic cane sugar
- $1/2$ cup maple syrup
- 1 cup raw cashews
- 3 tsp cinnamon
- $1/2$ tsp salt
- 6 ice cubes
- 2 cups cooked pumpkin or 796 ml canned pumpkin

Prepare crust recipe. Place gelatin and $3/4$ cup water in a blender and soak for 1 minute.

Pour 1 cup boiling water over soaked mixture and blend briefly to dissolve gelatin.

Add sugar, maple syrup, cashews, cinnamon and salt to blender and liquefy until creamy. Add ice cubes to the blender until the mixture reaches the 4 cup mark. Blend well.

Add pumpkin and blend until smooth. Pour blended mixture over your favourite baked crumb crust. Refrigerate overnight. Serve topped with Whipped Coconut Cream (see recipe page 253). Fits a 10 inch springform pan.

Serves 10

Queen Elizabeth Cake

- 1 cup chopped dates
- 1 cup boiling water
- 1 tsp baking soda
- 1 1/2 cups flour
- 2 tsp baking powder
- 1/4 tsp salt
- 1/2 cup chopped walnuts
- 1/4 cup organic cane sugar
- 1/4 cup maple syrup
- 1/4 cup non-dairy butter
- 1/4 cup of dessert tofu

Mix the dates, boiling water and soda. Let stand until cool. Stir flour, baking powder, salt and walnuts together.

Cream the sugar, maple syrup and non-dairy butter. Stir in dessert tofu.
Add the creamed mixture and dry ingredients. Mix well. Stir in the dates.
Bake in a 9 x 13 inch oiled cake pan at 350° F for 30-35 minutes.
Spread cake with topping and broil 3 inches below broiler on low heat until topping bubbles all over, being careful not to burn.

Topping for Queen Elizabeth Cake

- 1 Tbsp non-dairy butter
- 1/4 cup organic cane sugar
- 1/4 cup maple syrup
- 1 heaping cup of shredded sweetened coconut

Mix all ingredients together in a pot. Boil until the sugar is dissolved.
Remove from heat and drizzle over cake.
Cool topping on cake before serving.

Sesame Fingers

- 1 1/2 cups raw sesame seeds
- 3/4 cups fine, unsweetened coconut
- 1/2 cup peanut butter
- 1/4 cup liquid honey or maple syrup
- 1/4 cup organic cane sugar
- 1 tsp vanilla
- 1/2 tsp salt
- 1/2 cup finely chopped walnuts or pecans

Preheat oven to 300° F.

In a large bowl, mix all ingredients together until a thick batter forms.
Press the batter, about 1/2 inch thick, on a baking sheet lined with parchment paper.

Bake for about 30 minutes or until golden brown. While warm, use a sharp knife to slice into finger shapes about 3 inches long. Separate slightly as fingers tend to stick together as they cool.

Makes 12 fingers

Tomato Soup Cake

- 1/3-1/2 cup grape seed oil
- 2/3 cup organic cane sugar
- 1/4 cup dessert tofu
- 1 can condensed tomato soup
- 1/2 cup water
- 1 tsp soda
- 2 1/2 -3 cups unbleached flour
- 1/2 tsp salt
- 3 tsp baking powder
- 1/2 tsp cinnamon
- 1/2 tsp cloves
- 1 1/2 tsp ground nutmeg
- 1 1/2 cup raisins (rinsed and drained)
- 1 1/2 cup walnuts

Mix oil, sugar and tofu. Stir in tomato soup and water.

Mix dry ingredients together. Stir into wet ingredients. Add raisins and walnuts. Mix well.

Bake at 350° F for 45-50 minutes, in a 9 x 13 inch oiled pan.

Tropical Banana Cream Pie

Crust:

- 1 cup graham wafers, finely crushed
- 1/2 cup chopped walnuts
- 1/4 cup oats
- 1/4 cup organic sugar cane
- 4 Tbsp grape seed oil or butter substitute

Filling:

- 1-8 oz container soy cream cheese
- 1/3 cup dry sweetener of choice
- 2 -4 oz cans crushed pineapple, drained and patted dry
- 3 bananas
- 2 1/2 cups tofu milk (or milk of choice)
- 1 package vanilla pudding mix
- 1 1/2 cup Whipped Coconut Cream (see recipe page 253)
- fresh fruit or roasted coconut or pecans for topping

Mix together dry ingredients. Rub oil into mixture.
Spread onto an 8 x 8 inch oiled pan.
Bake at 350° F for 8 minutes or until lightly browned.
Cool.

Cream sugar and cream cheese together and set aside.
Combine tofu milk and pudding mix. Bring to boil slowly on medium heat.
Cool thoroughly (best to make the night before).
Fold in Whipped Coconut Cream.

Spread cream cheese mixture over baked crust.
Top with crushed pineapple.
Slice bananas and arrange over pineapple.
Spread chilled pudding and cream mixture carefully on top of bananas.
Place in fridge and chill for at least 5 hours.

Note: As an alternative to the pudding mix, use Nettie's Coconut Cream Pie Filling, vanilla flavoured.

Serves 8

Walnut Pie Crust

- 1 cup finely ground walnuts
- 1/2 cup flour
- 1/4 cup organic cane sugar
- pinch of salt
- 1/4 cup grape seed oil

Mix dry ingredients. Add the oil until mixture binds when squeezed. More oil may be needed. Press into pie pan and bake at 350° F for 15 minutes or until golden brown.

Variation: Use almonds, pecans, or hazelnuts to replace walnuts.

Whipped Coconut Cream
Our substitute for whipped cream.

- 1-398 ml can coconut milk (use a product with 12 g fat content)
- 3 Tbsp maple syrup or 1 Tbsp dry sweetener of choice
- vanilla to taste

Chill coconut milk until very cold. (It is handy to always keep a can refrigerated).

Open can and scoop out solidified coconut milk. (Do not add the liquid at the bottom of the can.)
Add it to a bowl with the sweetener and vanilla.

Whip mixture at top speed until thick like whipped cream.

Note: If coconut milk does not thicken (which sometimes happens) sprinkle 1/2 tsp instant clear gel (see Glossary) into coconut and continue to whip.

Glossary of Ingredients & Vegetarian Food Staples

Baking Ingredients

- Almond flavouring
- Baking powder (alum free)
- Baking soda
- Carob powder and chips (vegan)
- Chocolate powder and chips (vegan)
- Cinnamon
- Dessert tofu
- Egg replacement powder
- Gelatin powder (vegetable-based) made with carrageen (Irish moss)
- Instant clear gel (cold-liquid thickener)
- Maple extract
- Minute tapioca
- Molasses
- Phyllo pastry
- Tapioca starch
- Vanilla
- Whole cloves

Dried Fruits

- Apricots
- Cranberries
- Dates
- Mango
- Papaya
- Pineapple
- Raisins

Meat Substitutes

- Gluten strips, or Seitan beef or chicken type – use in stir fry and stews
- Tofu dessert – original or flavoured
- Tofu - firm, medium, marinated and smoked
- Veggie breakfast and dinner sausages - usually soy or gluten based
- Veggie burgers - rice, soy or lentil based
- Veggie ground round, or chicken – to replace minced meat – soy based
- Veggie luncheon deli slices, tofu dogs

There are many meat substitutes available, if you choose to use them, in health food stores and grocery stores. During our cooking classes, we provide you with information on preferred products.

Fresh Herbs

- Fresh parsley, dill, basil, cilantro, garlic, ginger, chives, rosemary

Dairy Substitutes

- Almond Beverage
- Non-dairy butter - we use a polyunsaturated vegan product with non-gmo soy and canola
- Rice Dream
- Silk
- Soy beverage
- Soy mayonnaise
- Tofu drink mix (powder)
- Canned coconut milk - to replace whipped cream, use a product with 12 g fat content

Cheese

- Soy cheddar
- Soy cream cheese
- Soy feta
- Soy mozzarella
- Soy parmesan
- Soy sour cream

Flours and Grains

- Bread yeast (quick rising)
- Brown rice
- Bulgur
- Cornmeal
- Couscous
- Garbanzo flour
- Gluten flour
- Kamut flour
- Lentils
- Millet
- Nutritional yeast
- Oats – quick and old-fashioned
- Quinoa – can be substituted for rice or bulgur in recipes
- Rye flour
- Soy flour
- Spelt flour
- Unbleached white flour
- Wheat germ
- Whole wheat flour

Nuts and Seeds

- Almonds
- Cashews - raw
- Coconut - unsweetened
- Flaxseed
- Pecans
- Pine nuts
- Pistachios
- Pumpkin seeds - unsalted
- Sesame seeds
- Sunflower seeds - unsalted
- Walnuts

Nut Butters

- Almond butter
- Cashew butter
- Peanut butter
- Tahini sesame butter

Oils - Vinegars

- Apple cider vinegar
- Balsamic vinegar
- Coconut oil
- Grape seed oil
- Olive oil - extra virgin and virgin
- Peanut oil
- Raspberry vinegar
- Red and white wine vinegar

- Rice wine vinegar
- Roasted sesame oil
- Vegetable oil spray

Sugars

- Agave nectar
- Brown rice syrup
- Date sugar
- Fructose sugar
- Honey
- Maple syrup
- Organic cane sugar
- Stevia
- Sucanat

Canned Goods and Condiments

- Beans
- Black
- Garbanzo
- Kidney
- Navy
- Pinto
- Soy

Miscellaneous

- Artichoke hearts – canned
- Black bean sauce
- Braggs Amino
- Capers
- Chilli sauce – Asian or Thai

- Chipotle canned peppers
- Curry paste – Indian or Thai, mild, medium or hot
- Hoisin sauce
- Mustards: Dijon, gourmet blends, ballpark
- Olives: Kalamata, gourmet blends
- Pears, canned
- Pickles
- Pineapple, canned
- Salsa
- Sodium reduced soy sauce
- Sun-dried tomatoes (oil packed)
- Sweet chilli sauce
- Tamari soy sauce
- Tomato juice
- Tomato paste
- Tomatoes
- V8 juice

Pasta and Wraps

- Chinese eggless noodles
- Kamut pasta
- Spelt pasta
- Whole wheat – Fettuccine
             Fusili
             Lasagne
             Macaroni
             Rotini
             Spaghetti
- Rice paper for wraps
- Rice noodles
- Tortilla wraps – variety of flavours and sizes

Seasonings

- Bay leaves
- Basil – dried
- Cayenne pepper
- Chicken style soup base – vegetarian
- Chilli powder
- Chipotle powder
- Coriander
- Cumin
- Curry paste
- Curry powder
- Dill – dried
- Five Spice Chinese Seasoning
- Garlic powder
- Garam Masala Indian Seasoning
- Garlic Plus – dried vegetable seasoning
- Greek dried vegetable seasoning
- Grilled Vegetable – dried vegetable seasoning
- Herbamare – aromatic sea salt
- Italian dried vegetable seasoning
- Lemon and Herbs – dried vegetable seasoning
- Mrs. Dash – vegetable seasoning
- Mustard seeds
- Nutmeg - whole
- Onion powder
- Oregano – dried
- Paprika – Hungarian sweet/hot
- Paprika – smoked
- Roasted Garlic and Peppers dried vegetable seasoning
- Rosemary – dried
- Sage – dried
- Sea salt

• Soup Bases – we use a vegan product that is transfat, wheat and gluten
   free. It comes in chicken, beef, onion and vegetable bases.

• Spike seasoning
• Turmeric

Cooking Terms

Al Dente	A term that means, "To cook to the teeth" or until barely tender, but still firm.
Bake	To cook by dry heat, either covered or uncovered in an oven, or oven type appliance.
Beat	To make a mixture smooth by introducing air with a brisk motion using a spoon or electric beaters.
Blanching	Plunging a food into boiling water for a few minutes (the time varies for each recipe). The food is then remove and generally placed in cold water to stop the cooking process. The purpose is to loosen the skin of a vegetable or fruit, to set the colour of a vegetable or to partially cook a food in prepa ration for later completion of a dish.
Blend	To combine two or more ingredients thoroughly.
Boil	To heat liquid until bubbles continuously break on the surface.
Broil	To cook by direct heat under a broiler in the oven.
Caramelize	To cook until food turns a light brown colour as in onions or as in sugar.
Chiffonade	To slice fine as in rolling fresh leaves of herbs together and slicing.
Chop	To cut food into small pieces.
Correct the Seasoning	When a dish is completed, a cook should always taste it before serving. To correct the seasoning, simply means to check for salt, pepper or herbs to make sure the dish has turned out as expected. A little correction at the last minute may be necessary.

Cream	To combine fat with sugar until mixture is light and fluffy.
Cube	To cut food into cubes about ½-inch thick
Dash	Generally means, "To taste" such as a dash of salt or cayenne.
Dice	To make small cubes about 1/4-inch
Flute	To make decorative indentations around edges of pastries, fruits or vegetables.
Fold	To combine ingredients using a spoon or rubber spatula. Go down through the mixture on the far side of the bowl; bring the spoon across the bottom, turning the mixture over while turning the bowl. Repeat until mixture is combined.
Fry	To cook in hot oil making sure oil comes to temperature before adding food, but making sure that oil doesn't smoke.
Glaze	To coat with a smooth mixture to give food a glossy appearance.
Julienne	To cut vegetables or fruit into long match like strips - length varies according to recipe.
Knead	To manipulate with a pressing motion accompanied by folding and stretching. For yeast bread, fold dough towards you; push dough away using the heel of your hand. Rotate 1/4, turn and repeat. For tea biscuits or scones, the kneading process is less vigorous and takes only several turns.
Marinate	To let food sit in a seasoned sauce called a marinade. It increases flavour and tenderizes a food.
Membrane	The fibre that sections citrus fruits. To remove the Membrane, peel the pith from the fruit and slice the Sections of fruit from the membrane.
Mince	To chop into very small pieces, smaller than a dice. Herbs are usually minced.

Mirepoix	A mixture of onion, celery, carrots, used in combination for soups and stews.
Mix	To combine ingredients until evenly distributed.
Parboil	To cook food in a boiling liquid until partially done. Cooking is usually completed by another method.
Pare	To remove outer covering of fruit or vegetable.
Pinch	Also called a dash and equals about 1/6 tsp.
Pith	The white membrane under the skin of citrus fruits. A recipe may call to remove all the pith.
Poach	To cook slowly in simmering liquid.
Proof	To activate yeast with liquid and sometimes flour, yeast and liquid prior to kneading dough.
Purée	To put food through a sieve, blender or processor to produce a thick pulp.
Reconstitute	A procedure used for preparing dried foods. The product is soaked for a time usually in water. The water is absorbed by the food and restores it almost to its original state. Examples are sundries tomato, dried mushrooms or raisins.
Reducing	Boiling a sauce or liquid over heat until it's reduced in volume. The result is very rich, concentrated flavours.
Roux	A blend of oil or butter and flour used to thicken sauces or gravies. The oil and flour are mixed in equal amounts over heat. If a white roux is desired, the cooking is done over low heat for a few minutes. If a brown roux is desired, the flour and oil are cooked until lightly brown. The roux will thicken liquid it is added to.
Sauté	To brown or cook in a small amount of oil.

Simmer	To cook in liquid just below boiling point. Bubbles form slowly and burst before reaching the surface.
Smooth & Creamy	The texture you want your cashew or almond cream to be when you purée it. Any grit in the purée will produce a gritty sauce.
Stir Fry	A basic cooking method generally using a wok but a frying pan will work. The food is tossed about in a hot pan with very little oil. Not unlike sautéing.
Steam	To cook in a covered container above boiling water.
Steep	To let stand for a few minutes in water that has just been boiled it enhances flavour and colour.
Temper	To add warm liquid slowly to cold liquid so the mixture doesn't separate. Or as in chocolate, to melt the chocolate slowly from its solid state.
Toss	To mix ingredients lightly with a lifting motion as in salad or pasta.
Whip	To beat rapidly with a wire whisk beater or mixer to incorporate air and increase volume.
Zest	To use a knife or zesting tool to remove a very thin outer layer of citrus fruit.

Sectional Index

Breakfast

Breads & Quick Breads

Salads and Dressings

Dips, Spreads and Sauces

Soups

Vegetables

Entrees

Rice Recipes

Desserts

Alphabetical Index